TEACHER GUIDE

Includes ~~Student~~ ~~Worksheets~~ ~~Weekly Schedule~~

9th–12th Grade

History ~~Answer Key~~

American History

MasterBooks® CURRICULUM

Author: Jim Stobaugh

Master Books Creative Team:

Editor: Craig Froman

Design: Terry White

Cover Design: Diana Bogardus

Copy Editors:
Judy Lewis
Willow Meek

Curriculum Review:
Kristen Pratt
Laura Welch
Diana Bogardus

First printing: March 2012
Fifth revised printing: May 2021

Master Books®, P.O. Box 726, Green Forest, AR 72638

Master Books® is a division of the New Leaf Publishing Group, Inc.

ISBN: 978-0-89051-643-0
ISBN: 978-1-61458-137-6 (digital)

Unless otherwise noted, Scripture quotations are from the New King James Version of the Bible.

Printed in the United States of America

Please visit our website for other great titles:
www.masterbooks.com

About the Author:

James P. Stobaugh and his wife, Karen, have homeschooled their four children since 1985. They have a growing ministry, For Such a Time As This Ministries, committed to challenging this generation to change its world for Christ. Dr. Stobaugh is an ordained pastor, a certified secondary teacher, and an SAT coach. His academic credentials include: BA, cum laude Vanderbilt University; Teacher Certification, Peabody College for Teachers; MA, Rutgers University; MDiv, Princeton Theological Seminary; Merrill Fellow, Harvard University; DMin Gordon Conwell Seminary.

Your reputation as a publisher is stellar. It is a blessing knowing anything I purchase from you is going to be worth every penny!

—Cheri ★ ★ ★ ★ ★

Last year we found Master Books and it has made a HUGE difference.

—Melanie ★ ★ ★ ★ ★

We love Master Books and the way it's set up for easy planning!

—Melissa ★ ★ ★ ★ ★

You have done a great job. MASTER BOOKS ROCKS!

—Stephanie ★ ★ ★ ★ ★

Physically high-quality, Biblically faithful, and well-written.

—Danika ★ ★ ★ ★ ★

Best books ever. Their illustrations are captivating and content amazing!

—Kathy ★ ★ ★ ★ ★

Affordable
Flexible
Faith Building

Table of Contents

History Is the Remembering: There are two primary points of view about the way history is formed… and thus remembered. One says that history is nothing more than arbitrary events connected by happenstance. The opposite point of view, this author's point of view, argues that there is a design, purpose, or pattern in history. As a matter of fact, history is nothing more or less than an unfolding of God's plan for the world.

Know that history is alive, full of interesting, glorious, and useful things, and terribly relevant to all of us. To be a true history, an account of the past must not only retell what happened but must also relate events and people to each other. It must inquire into causes and effects. It must try to discern falsehood in the old records, such as attempts of historical figures to make them look better than they really were. It must also present the evidence on which its findings are based.

How this course has been developed:

1. **Chapters:** This course has 34 chapters of study.

2. **Lessons:** Each chapter has four lessons based on the student book, taking approximately 30 to 45 minutes each. The teacher guide has a daily schedule of readings, worksheets, and quarterly exams.

3. **Quarterly exams:** The final lesson of each quarter is the exam. Students are not to use their text to answer these questions.

4. **Student responsibility:** Responsibility to complete this course is on the student. Students are to complete the readings every day, handing their responses to a parent or teacher for evaluation. This course is designed for the student to practice independent learning.

5. **Grading:** A parent or teacher may choose to grade exams only or worksheets and exams. A teacher may also change or eliminate an assignment or part of an assignment at their discretion. Answers are available at the end of the teacher guide for all assignments. You may use the standard system (90-100 = A, 80-89 = B, 70-79 = C, 60-69 = D, below 60 = F), or you may use your own personal grading system. All worksheets and exams are valued at 100 possible points.

6. **Research note:** Throughout the course, students will at times be given assignments to research content from sources outside the primary course text. With permission of the teacher, this might include library sources or online resources. A teacher may also elect to make these assignments optional.

7. **Friday Project Day:** The purpose of these projects (one per semester) will be to compel students to utilize the themes of the course to better understand history on a larger scale. As such, you can select from a range of projects, finding one best suited to your interests. A few example prompts and creative project ideas will be given, but, at the instructor's discretion, any creative project or prompt can be used that deals with the themes of the course. All essays should be five pages or longer and use no less than three chapters from the book, as well as three outside sources.

Features: The suggested weekly schedule enclosed has easy-to-manage lessons that guide the reading, worksheets, and all assessments. The pages of this guide are perforated and three-hole punched so materials are easy to tear out, hand out, grade, and store. Teachers are encouraged to adjust the schedule and materials needed in order to best work within their unique educational program.

History Notes: *American History* invites students to be historians. Students look at the sources and scholarship available and make a decision. They must know and accept that our understanding of the past can change according to new scholarship discoveries. Therefore, as new sources are discovered, and old ones reexamined, students understand that theories of history may change. This course enables students to commit themselves to the task of examining these theories and primary source material and ultimately to form their own theories of history. Let it be your goal to make the theories of historical events personal and contemporary.

	Approximately 30–45 minutes per lesson, five days a week
	Includes answer keys for activity sheets and reviews
	Activity sheets for each chapter
	Reviews are included to help reinforce learning and provide assessment opportunities.
	Designed for grades 9 to 12 in a one-year history course

Course Objectives: Students completing this course will

- Examine history through the writings contained in original source documents
- Compare and contrast the cultures of early Native peoples with the first Europeans
- Observe colonial life and the causes of the American Revolution
- Discover the roots of revivalism, as well as the Christian worldview so prominent in the founding of the nation
- Study current-day social issues that shape the United States as a nation, including civil rights, ecology, and abortion
- Learn about the rise of the U.S. as a global leader through war and peace

Comparative Worldviews

	God	Man	Sin	Authority/Revelation	Salvation
Agnosticism	Deny the certainty of the existence of God, but in various forms. They would generally reject the idea of Divinity, the Trinity, and Jesus as the Son of God or Savior.	Generally accept an evolutionary view of man. No concept of a sinful nature. Man is a mortal being and part of the animal kingdom, with no particularly special role in the universe.	Sin is not generally a part of agnostic thinking, though some would adopt certain cultural taboos. There is no view to judgment of sin since they reject knowledge of deity.	Mostly reliant on materialistic, empirical thinking with human reasoning coupled with sense perception being the ultimate standard of truth. Reject any form of supernatural revelation, including the Bible.	There is no concept of salvation apart from some cultural ideas. Reject the need of Jesus as Savior.
Biblical Truth	God is triune, existing in three persons of the Godhead — Father, Son, and Holy Spirit; God is eternal and transcendent; the Son took on flesh to dwell on earth.	Man is created in the image of God; mankind is fallen as a result of Adam's sin; man is unable to do good and please God on his own.	Any thought or action that is contrary to the will of God as revealed in the Bible.	God and His revelation of Himself in the 66 books of the Bible.	Salvation is possible through the substitutionary atonement of Jesus on the Cross and His Resurrection; individuals receive salvation by repentance and faith in Jesus' work on their behalf; works have no merit for salvation; salvation is a free gift received by God's grace alone.
Communism	Deny the existence of God. Man is viewed as the supreme being.	Man is the measure of all things and basically good. Certain individuals are intended to lead others, but there is broad equality in humanity.	Sin is not a prominent concept. Right and wrong are relative to achieving the goals of the state.	The writings of various authors are appealed to, though there is no notion of an authoritative revelation..	The goal of humanity is to achieve equality. There is no view to an afterlife.
Deism	A distant deity or force that has no intimate interaction with the world.	A rational being who directs his own destiny.	Varies by individual; generally rejected as any absolute standard.	Deny any special revelation from God; acknowledge natural law discerned by human reason and practice.	Varies by individual; some acknowledge an afterlife.

	God	Man	Sin	Authority/Revelation	Salvation
Secular Humanism	Deny the existence of God or any divine being; or they acknowledge a god may exist, but he is not involved in the affairs of man. Believe nature is selfexisting. Reject Jesus as Savior or God.	All men are the result of "unguided evolutionary change" and have no existence beyond this earthly life. The goal of man is to maximize his own pleasure without harming others. Man is a social animal.	Sin is denied as any type of moral absolute. "Ethical values" are based in "human welfare" and change with new experience and knowledge.	Man is the measure of all things. Naturalism, materialism, and rationalism are key concepts in determining truth. Scientific inquiry is the highest pursuit of truth.	There is no belief in an afterlife and no need to consider salvation since death is the end.
Islam	Deny the Trinity; believe Allah is the only god (monotheistic) and that Jesus is not the Son of God, but a prophet; Allah is transcendent and removed from mankind.	Man is the highest creature made by Allah and is able to do good with his free will, though he needs guidance from Allah's prophets.	Transgression of Allah's will as revealed in the Quran and Hadith; no concept of original sin corrupting mankind.	The Bible is viewed as a revelation from God that has been corrupted, but the revelations of Muhammad in the Quran supersede the Bible.	Each person will be judged by Allah for his or her own actions; there is no concept of a mediator or Savior and they deny that Jesus died on the Cross; martyrs receive entrance into Paradise.
Judaism	Deny the Trinity; there is only one God; Jesus is not the Son of God or the Messiah; the Holy Spirit is not a person.	Man is created in the image of God; mankind is fallen as a result of Adam's sin; man is able to attain perfection.	Disobeying the laws prescribed in the Old Testament.	39 books of the Old Testament; Talmud; various rabbis and traditions.	Salvation is possible through the obedience of the individual to biblical and rabbinical laws; atonement is accomplished through personal acts of sacrifice and penitence.
Postmodernism	Deny the exclusivity of the God of the Bible. Various positions exist, but all would deny the exclusivity of Jesus as Savior.	All men are able to determine truth on their own. Various positions exist on the nature of man, but most would view man as basically good.	Sin is a relative concept and generally denied. The Bible cannot be seen as the absolute authority on what is sinful.	Holds a humanistic view of truth, looking to man as the source of truth.	Most would hold the position that if there is an afterlife, there are many different paths to get there.

First Semester Suggested Daily Schedule

Date	Day	Assignment	Due Date	✓	Grade
		First Semester — First Quarter			
Week 1	Day 1	Chapter 1: Natives of the New World Read Lesson 1 — War of the Worldviews Student Book (SB) Complete Assignment Page 19 Teacher Guide (TG)			
	Day 2	Read Lesson 2 — North American Indigenous People Groups (SB) Complete Assignment Page 20 (TG)			
	Day 3	Read Lesson 3 — South-Central American Indigenous People Groups (SB) Complete Assignment Page 21 (TG)			
	Day 4	Read Lesson 4 — Columbus, Conquistadors, and Colonization (SB) Complete Assignment Page 22 (TG)			
	Day 5	Semester 1 Writing Project Pages 23-24 (TG)			
Week 2	Day 6	Chapter 2: Slavery and Religious Freedom Read Lesson 1 — French Exploration and Colonization (SB) Complete Assignment Page 25 (TG)			
	Day 7	Read Lesson 2 — The Virginia Company (SB) Complete Assignment Page 26 (TG)			
	Day 8	Read Lesson 3 — Chattel Slavery Comes to the New World (SB) Complete Assignment Page 27 (TG)			
	Day 9	Read Lesson 4 — Other Explorers (SB) Complete Assignment Page 28 (TG)			
	Day 10	Semester 1 Writing Project Page 29 (TG)			
Week 3	Day 11	Chapter 3: Pilgrims and Puritans Read Lesson 1 — Pilgrims (SB) Complete Assignment Page 31 (TG)			
	Day 12	Read Lesson 2 — The Puritans: A Holy Experiment (SB) Complete Assignment Page 32 (TG)			
	Day 13	Read Lesson 3 — Other Colonies (SB) Complete Assignment Page 33 (TG)			
	Day 14	Read Lesson 4 — Historical Debate and Worldview (SB) Complete Assignment Page 34 (TG)			
	Day 15	Semester 1 Writing Project Page 35 (TG)			
Week 4	Day 16	Chapter 4: Colonial Life Read Lesson 1 — Colonial Women (SB) Complete Assignment Page 37 (TG)			
	Day 17	Read Lesson 2 — The First Great Awakening (SB) Complete Assignment Page 38 (TG)			
	Day 18	Read Lesson 3 — The American University: An Essay (SB) Complete Assignment Page 39 (TG)			
	Day 19	Read Lesson 4 — Philosophers and Worldviews (SB) Complete Assignment Page 40 (TG)			
	Day 20	Semester 1 Writing Project Page 41 (TG)			

Date	Day	Assignment	Due Date	✓	Grade
Week 5	Day 21	**Chapter 5: Causes of the American Revolution** Read Lesson 1 — Colonial Period (SB) Complete Assignment Page 43 (TG)			
	Day 22	Read Lesson 2 — The Road to Revolution (SB) Complete Assignment Page 44 (TG)			
	Day 23	Read Lesson 3 — The French and Indian War (SB) Complete Assignment Page 45 (TG)			
	Day 24	Read Lesson 4 — George Washington (SB) Complete Assignment Page 46 (TG)			
	Day 25	Semester 1 Writing Project Page 47 (TG)			
Week 6	Day 26	**Chapter 6: Patriots and Revolution** Read Lesson 1 — The Coming Conflict (SB) Complete Assignment Page 49 (TG)			
	Day 27	Read Lesson 2 — The War (SB) Complete Assignment Page 50 (TG)			
	Day 28	Read Lesson 3 — Abigail Adams (SB) Complete Assignment Page 51 (TG)			
	Day 29	Read Lesson 4 — Historical Debate: American Revolution (SB) Complete Assignment Page 52 (TG)			
	Day 30	Semester 1 Writing Project Page 53 (TG)			
Week 7	Day 31	**Chapter 7: U.S. Constitution** Read Lesson 1 — The Constitution: Part One (SB) Complete Assignment Page 55 (TG)			
	Day 32	Read Lesson 2 — The Constitution: Part Two (SB) Complete Assignment Page 56 (TG)			
	Day 33	Read Lesson 3 — Philosophers and Worldviews (SB) Complete Assignment Page 57 (TG)			
	Day 34	Read Lesson 4 — Historical Debate: The Constitution (SB) Complete Assignment Page 58 (TG)			
	Day 35	Semester 1 Writing Project Page 59 (TG)			
Week 8	Day 36	**Chapter 8: Nationalism** Read Lesson 1 — A Peaceful Revolution (SB) Complete Assignment Page 61 (TG)			
	Day 37	Read Lesson 2 — An Era of Good Feeling (SB) Complete Assignment Page 62 (TG)			
	Day 38	Read Lesson 3 — History Maker: John Quincy Adams (SB) Complete Assignment Page 63 (TG)			
	Day 39	Read Lesson 4 — Historical Debate: National Period (SB) Complete Assignment Page 64 (TG)			
	Day 40	Semester 1 Writing Project Page 65 (TG)			

Date	Day	Assignment	Due Date	✓	Grade
Week 9	Day 41	Chapter 9: Democracy and New Governments Read Lesson 1 — Philosophers and Worldviews (SB) Complete Assignment Page 67 (TG)			
	Day 42	Read Lesson 2 — The Rise of the American Political Tradition (SB) Complete Assignment Page 68 (TG)			
	Day 43	Read Lesson 3 — Jacksonian Democracy (SB) Complete Assignment Page 69 (TG)			
	Day 44	Read Lesson 4 — History Maker: Daniel Webster (SB) Complete Assignment Page 70 (TG)			
	Day 45	**Quarterly Exam 1** Pages 225-226 (TG) Semester 1 Writing Project Page 71 (TG)			
First Semester — Second Quarter					
Week 1	Day 46	Chapter 10: Age of Reform Read Lesson 1 — Prison Reform (SB) Complete Assignment Page 73 (TG)			
	Day 47	Read Lesson 2 — The Rights of Women and the Mentally Challenged (SB) Complete Assignment Page 74 (TG)			
	Day 48	Read Lesson 3 — History Maker: Dorothea Dix (SB) Complete Assignment Page 75 (TG)			
	Day 49	Read Lesson 4 — Philosophers and Worldviews (SB) Complete Assignment Page 76 (TG)			
	Day 50	Semester 1 Writing Project Page 77 (TG)			
Week 2	Day 51	Chapter 11: Antebellum Slavery Read Lesson 1 — Slavery (SB) Complete Assignment Page 79 (TG)			
	Day 52	Read Lesson 2 — History Maker: Harriet Tubman (SB) Complete Assignment Page 80 (TG)			
	Day 53	Read Lesson 3 — Historical Debate (SB) Complete Assignment Page 81 (TG)			
	Day 54	Read Lesson 4 — Philosophers and Worldviews (SB) Complete Assignment Page 82 (TG)			
	Day 55	Semester 1 Writing Project Page 83 (TG)			
Week 3	Day 56	Chapter 12: Revivalism Read Lesson 1 — Come to the Water: American Revivalism (SB) Complete Assignment Page 85 (TG)			
	Day 57	Read Lesson 2 — Revivalism (SB) Complete Assignment Page 86 (TG)			
	Day 58	Read Lesson 3 — A Contemporary Account of a Revival (SB) Complete Assignment Page 87 (TG)			
	Day 59	Read Lesson 4 — History Maker: Charles Finney (SB) Complete Assignment Page 88 (TG)			
	Day 60	Semester 1 Writing Project Page 89 (TG)			

Date	Day	Assignment	Due Date	✓	Grade
Week 4	Day 61	Chapter 13: Causes of the American Civil War Read Lesson 1 — The Coming Crisis: Part One (SB) Complete Assignment Page 91 (TG)			
	Day 62	Read Lesson 2 — The Coming Crisis: Part Two (SB) Complete Assignment Page 92 (TG)			
	Day 63	Read Lesson 3 — The Coming Crisis: Part Three (SB) Complete Assignment Page 93 (TG)			
	Day 64	Read Lesson 4 — Philosophers and Worldviews (SB) Complete Assignment Page 94 (TG)			
	Day 65	Semester 1 Writing Project Page 95 (TG)			
Week 5	Day 66	Chapter 14: The American Civil War Read Lesson 1 — Presidents (SB) Complete Assignment Page 97 (TG)			
	Day 67	Read Lesson 2 — The American Civil War (SB) Complete Assignment Page 98 (TG)			
	Day 68	Read Lesson 3 — The Results of the American Civil War (SB) Complete Assignment Page 99 (TG)			
	Day 69	Read Lesson 4 — History Maker: Abraham Lincoln (SB) Complete Assignment Page 100 (TG)			
	Day 70	Semester 1 Writing Project Page 101 (TG)			
Week 6	Day 71	Chapter 15: Reconstruction Read Lesson 1 — Robert E. Lee (SB) Complete Assignment Page 103 (TG)			
	Day 72	Read Lesson 2 — Reconstruction (SB) Complete Assignment Page 104 (TG)			
	Day 73	Read Lesson 3 — More Questions on Reconstruction (SB) Complete Assignment Page 105 (TG)			
	Day 74	Read Lesson 4 — Race Mixing (SB) Complete Assignment Page 106 (TG)			
	Day 75	Semester 1 Writing Project Page 107 (TG)			
Week 7	Day 76	Chapter 16: Reconstruction: Primary Sources Read Lesson 1 — Andrew Johnson (SB) Complete Assignment Page 109 (TG)			
	Day 77	Read Lesson 2 — Primary Sources (SB) Complete Assignment Page 110 (TG)			
	Day 78	Read Lesson 3 — Villain or Hero? (SB) Complete Assignment Page 111 (TG)			
	Day 79	Read Lesson 4 — Philosophers and Worldviews (SB) Complete Assignment Page 112 (TG)			
	Day 80	Semester 1 Writing Project Page 113 (TG)			

Date	Day	Assignment	Due Date	✓	Grade
Week 8	Day 81	Chapter 17: Immigration Read Lesson 1 — The Home of the Free (SB) Complete Assignment Page 115 (TG)			
	Day 82	Read Lesson 2 — Immigration (SB) Complete Assignment Page 116 (TG)			
	Day 83	Read Lesson 3 — Albert Einstein (SB) Complete Assignment Page 117 (TG)			
	Day 84	Read Lesson 4 — Karl Marx (SB) Complete Assignment Page 118 (TG)			
	Day 85	Semester 1 Writing Project Page 119 (TG)			
Week 9	Day 86	Chapter 18: The Gilded Age Read Lesson 1 — The Gilded Age (SB) Complete Assignment Page 121 (TG)			
	Day 87	Read Lesson 2 — American Labor Movement (SB) Complete Assignment Page 122 (TG)			
	Day 88	Read Lesson 3 — Historical Debate (SB) Complete Assignment Page 123 (TG)			
	Day 89	Read Lesson 4 — Vladimir Ilyich Lenin (SB) Complete Assignment Page 124 (TG)			
	Day 90	**Quarterly Exam 2** Pages 227–228 (TG)			
		Midterm Grade			

Second Semester Suggested Daily Schedule

Date	Day	Assignment	Due Date	✓	Grade
		Second Semester — Third Quarter			
Week 1	Day 91	Chapter 19: The Gilded Age: Problems Read Lesson 1 — Social Welfare and Christianity (SB) Complete Assignment Page 127 (TG)			
	Day 92	Read Lesson 2 — Pierre Joseph Proudhon (SB) Complete Assignment Page 128 (TG)			
	Day 93	Read Lesson 3 — A Case Study: The Johnstown Flood (SB) Complete Assignment Page 129 (TG)			
	Day 94	Read Lesson 4 — William Jennings Bryan (SB) Complete Assignment Page 130 (TG)			
	Day 95	Semester 2 Writing Project Pages 131–132 (TG)			
Week 2	Day 96	Chapter 20: The Wild West Read Lesson 1 — The Wild West (SB) Complete Assignment Page 133 (TG)			
	Day 97	Read Lesson 2 — Native Americans (SB) Complete Assignment Page 134 (TG)			
	Day 98	Read Lesson 3 — Lawmen and Outlaws (SB) Complete Assignment Page 135 (TG)			
	Day 99	Read Lesson 4 — Frances Willard (SB) Complete Assignment Page 136 (TG)			
	Day 100	Semester 2 Writing Project Page 137 (TG)			
Week 3	Day 101	Chapter 21: African American History: The Great Migration Read Lesson 1 — The Great Migration (SB) Complete Assignment Page 139 (TG)			
	Day 102	Read Lesson 2 — Booker T. Washington (SB) Complete Assignment Page 140 (TG)			
	Day 103	Read Lesson 3 — Primary Sources (SB) Complete Assignment Page 141 (TG)			
	Day 104	Read Lesson 4 — Historical Debate (SB) Complete Assignment Page 142 (TG)			
	Day 105	Semester 2 Writing Project Page 143 (TG)			
Week 4	Day 106	Chapter 22: America Becomes a World Power Read Lesson 1 — American Becomes A World Power (SB) Complete Assignment Page 145 (TG)			
	Day 107	Read Lesson 2 — President Theodore Roosevelt (SB) Complete Assignment Page 146 (TG)			
	Day 108	Read Lesson 3 — Primary Sources (SB) Complete Assignment Page 147 (TG)			
	Day 109	Read Lesson 4 — More Primary Sources (SB) Complete Assignment Page 148 (TG)			
	Day 110	Semester 2 Writing Project Page 149 (TG)			

Date	Day	Assignment	Due Date	✓	Grade
Week 5	Day 111	Chapter 23: World War 1 and the Roaring '20s Read Lesson 1 — World War 1 (SB) Complete Assignment Page 151 (TG)			
	Day 112	Read Lesson 2 — Historical Debate (SB) Complete Assignment Page 152 (TG)			
	Day 113	Read Lesson 3 — Perils of Prosperity (SB) Complete Assignment Page 153 (TG)			
	Day 114	Read Lesson 4 — The Great Depression (SB) Complete Assignment Page 154 (TG)			
	Day 115	Semester 2 Writing Project Page 155 (TG)			
Week 6	Day 116	Chapter 24: American Life: 1900-1940 Read Lesson 1 — Billy Sunday (SB) Complete Assignment Page 157 (TG)			
	Day 117	Read Lesson 2 — Historical Debate (SB) Complete Assignment Page 158 (TG)			
	Day 118	Read Lesson 3 — Philosophers and Worldviews (SB) Complete Assignment Page 159 (TG)			
	Day 119	Read Lesson 4 — Oral History: Helen Parris Stobaugh (SB) Complete Assignment Page 160 (TG)			
	Day 120	Semester 2 Writing Project Page 161 (TG)			
Week 7	Day 121	Chapter 25: World War II and Beyond Read Lesson 1 — Remember Pearl Harbor (SB) Complete Assignment Page 163 (TG)			
	Day 122	Read Lesson 2 — The Holocaust (SB) Complete Assignment Page 164 (TG)			
	Day 123	Read Lesson 3 — The Cold War (SB) Complete Assignment Page 165 (TG)			
	Day 124	Read Lesson 4 — The Korean War (SB) Complete Assignment Page 166 (TG)			
	Day 125	Semester 2 Writing Project Page 167 (TG)			
Week 8	Day 126	Chapter 26: The Vietnam War Read Lesson 1 — War in Vietnam (SB) Complete Assignment Page 169 (TG)			
	Day 127	Read Lesson 2 — History Maker: Lech Walesa (SB) Complete Assignment Page 170 (TG)			
	Day 128	Read Lesson 3 — Historical Debate (SB) Complete Assignment Page 171 (TG)			
	Day 129	Read Lesson 4 — Philosophers and Worldviews (SB) Complete Assignment Page 172 (TG)			
	Day 130	Semester 2 Writing Project Page 173 (TG)			

Date	Day	Assignment	Due Date	✓	Grade
Week 9	Day 131	Chapter 27: African American History: Nationalism Read Lesson 1 — Black Nationalism (SB) Complete Assignment Page 175 (TG)			
	Day 132	Read Lesson 2 — Separatism (SB) Complete Assignment Page 176 (TG)			
	Day 133	Read Lesson 3 — Racial Anger (SB) Complete Assignment Page 177 (TG)			
	Day 134	Read Lesson 4 — Oral History (SB) Complete Assignment Page 178 (TG)			
	Day 135	**Quarterly Exam 3** Pages 229–230 (TG) Semester 2 Writing Project Page 179 (TG)			
Second Semester — Fourth Quarter					
Week 1	Day 136	Chapter 28: African American History: Free at Last Read Lesson 1 — History Maker: Martin Luther King Jr. (SB) Complete Assignment Page 181 (TG)			
	Day 137	Read Lesson 2 — Two Different Views (SB) Complete Assignment Page 182 (TG)			
	Day 138	Read Lesson 3 — The Welfare State (SB) Complete Assignment Page 183 (TG)			
	Day 139	Read Lesson 4 — Oral History (SB) Complete Assignment Page 184 (TG)			
	Day 140	Semester 2 Writing Project Page 185 (TG)			
Week 2	Day 141	Chapter 29: Culture Wars: 1950s to the Present Read Lesson 1 — Culture Wars: Part One (SB) Complete Assignment Page 187 (TG)			
	Day 142	Read Lesson 2 — Culture Wars: Part Two (SB) Complete Assignment Page 188 (TG)			
	Day 143	Read Lesson 3 — More Questions (SB) Complete Assignment Page 189 (TG)			
	Day 144	Read Lesson 4 — The Death of Outrage (SB) Complete Assignment Page 190 (TG)			
	Day 145	Semester 2 Writing Project Page 191 (TG)			
Week 3	Day 146	Chapter 30: Contemporary Social History Read Lesson 1 — A Case Study: Social History in the '50s (SB) Complete Assignment Page 193 (TG)			
	Day 147	Read Lesson 2 — Homeschooling (SB) Complete Assignment Page 194 (TG)			
	Day 148	Read Lesson 3 — "Peekaboo World" (SB) Complete Assignment Page 195 (TG)			
	Day 149	Read Lesson 4 — Billy Graham (SB) Complete Assignment Page 196 (TG)			
	Day 150	Semester 2 Writing Project Page 197 (TG)			

Date	Day	Assignment	Due Date	✓	Grade
Week 4	Day 151	Chapter 31: Late 20th Century Worldviews Read Lesson 1 — Philosophers and Worldview (SB) Complete Assignment Page 199 (TG)			
	Day 152	Read Lesson 2 — Charles Fuller (SB) Complete Assignment Page 200 (TG)			
	Day 153	Read Lesson 3 — Pax Americana (SB) Complete Assignment Page 201 (TG)			
	Day 154	Read Lesson 4 — The Next Twenty-Five Years (SB) Complete Assignment Page 202 (TG)			
	Day 155	Semester 2 Writing Project Page 203 (TG)			
Week 5	Day 156	Chapter 32: War on Terrorism Read Lesson 1 — The War on Terrorism (SB) Complete Assignment Page 205 (TG)			
	Day 157	Read Lesson 2 — The Koran (SB) Complete Assignment Page 206 (TG)			
	Day 158	Read Lesson 3 — A Twilight Struggle (SB) Complete Assignment Page 207 (TG)			
	Day 159	Read Lesson 4 — Historical Essay (SB) Complete Assignment Page 208 (TG)			
	Day 160	Semester 2 Writing Project Page 209 (TG)			
Week 6	Day 161	Chapter 33: Contemporary Issues: Part One Read Lesson 1 — Abortion (SB) Complete Assignment Page 211 (TG)			
	Day 162	Read Lesson 2 — Racial Reconciliation (SB) Complete Assignment Page 212 (TG)			
	Day 163	Read Lesson 3 — The Future of Homeschooling and Christian Education (SB) Complete Assignment Page 213 (TG)			
	Day 164	Read Lesson 4 — Christianity and Hip Hop (SB) Complete Assignment Page 214 (TG)			
	Day 165	Semester 2 Writing Project Page 215 (TG)			
Week 7	Day 166	Chapter 34: Contemporary Issues: Part Two Read Lesson 1 — Euthanasia (SB) Complete Assignment Page 217 (TG)			
	Day 167	Read Lesson 2 — Global Warming (SB) Complete Assignment Page 218 (TG)			
	Day 168	Read Lesson 3 — Healthcare (SB) Complete Assignment Page 219 (TG)			
	Day 169	Read Lesson 4 — Population Explosion (SB) Complete Assignment Page 220 (TG)			
	Day 170	**Quarterly Exam 4** Pages 231–232 (TG) Semester 2 Writing Project Page 221 (TG)			
		Semester Grade			

Daily Worksheets

for Use with

American History

Assignment (Each answer is worth 10 points.)

True / False:

1. Existentialism is an innately optimistic worldview. T/F

2. Evangelicals are not anti-intellectuals. T/F

3. Thomas Jefferson was a Romanticist. T/F

4. Christian Theism is growing in the 21st century. T/F

5. Absurdists don't care who or what is in control of the universe. T/F

Multiple Choice:

6. _____ is one of the most potent anti-Enlightenment movements in world history.
   (a) Evangelicalism
   (b) Existentialism
   (c) Roman Catholicism
   (d) Anti-intellectualism

7. _____ helps us make the critical decisions that will shape our future.
   (a) Evangelicalism
   (b) Homeschooling
   (c) Worldview
   (d) Enlightenment thinking

8. By side-stepping the Enlightenment, _____ has opened up a whole new arena for debate.
   (a) Evangelicalism
   (b) Christian homeschooling
   (c) Naturalism
   (d) Theism

Fill in the Blank:

9. A worldview is a way that a person understands, relates to, and responds from a _____ position that he embraces as his own.

10. Christian homeschooling posits that it is still important that we look beyond our experience for _____.

Assignment (Each answer is worth 10 points.)

True / False:

1. Roughly 10 to 90 million Native Americans inhabited America during the European arrival. T/F

2. The peace brokered by Pocahontas' marriage to John Rolfe was long-lasting. T/F

3. The Delaware people were some of the last Natives to meet the Europeans. T/F

4. The Iroquois were known as "the people of the longhouse." T/F

5. Powhatan ruled eight small tribes by the time the settlers arrived in 1607. T/F

Fill in the Blank:

6. The _____ were among the first Native people groups to come in contact with the Europeans.

7. On March 22, 1622, the _____ made the first, and perhaps most successful, attack to end European colonization on the North American continent.

8. Perhaps no Native American tribe was more influential in American history than the Iroquois _____.

9. The culture is identified by the distinctive _____ point, a flaked flint spear-point.

10. Jesuit, Anglican, and other missionaries brought new _____ to these indigenous people groups.

Assignment (Each answer is worth 10 points.)

True / False:

1. Drunkenness and promiscuity were favored by the Aztec culture. T/F

2. The Mayas exercised strong administrative control over their empire. T/F

3. Olmec culture was influential for the Mayas. T/F

4. The Mayas were skilled mathematicians and astronomers. T/F

5. The founder of the Incan dynasty was Cápac Yupanqui. T/F

Fill in the Blank:

6. Use of the road system was strictly limited to _____ and military business.

7. Most of those sacrificed by the Mayas were _____ from battle.

8. Practically every Incan man was a _____, producing his own food and clothing.

9. The Mayas developed an advanced _____ system.

10. The _____ culture is often regarded as the fostering influence behind the Mayan, Aztec, and other later societies.

Assignment (Each answer is worth 10 points.)

True / False:

1. The Viking settlements lasted for roughly 200 years. T/F

2. Columbus died without realizing he had not reached the East Indies. T/F

3. Vasco Nunez de Balboa was framed for treason by his friend. T/F

4. Ponce de Leon succeeded in his ventures. T/F

5. Pizzaro murdered Atahualpa during peace talks. T/F

Fill in the Blank:

6. Ponce de Leon named it Florida because he saw lots of _____.

7. The encomiendas, in truth, were a form of legalized _____.

8. The Vikings were the first _____ to settle in North America.

9. Christopher Columbus was largely schooled at _____.

10. Balboa was a Spanish conquistador and explorer who was the first European to see the eastern part of the _____ Ocean.

Semester One Friday Project

This is the beginning of your semester-long project, which you will be working on every Friday instead of a traditional lesson/worksheet. The purpose of this project will be to compel you to utilize the themes of the course to better understand history on a larger scope. As such, you can select from a range of projects, finding one best suited to your interests. A few example prompts and creative project ideas will be given, but, at your instructor's discretion, any creative project or prompt can be used that deals with the themes of the course. All essays will be five pages or longer and use no less than three chapters from the book, as well as three outside sources. For this first Friday, all that you need to do is select a project and begin gathering the materials required to write it.

Prompts:

#1

In the very first lesson, the author lays out eight worldviews. For this prompt, you will choose three people covered in the text (feel free to look ahead to favorite figures from history, provided you select from the fall term) and gather a source from the library or Internet about each. Spend time dissecting the worldview of each figure before developing a comparison to the biblical worldview found on the chart in the back of the student book and front of this teacher guide.

#2

The first half of American history thematically shows that people in power will often abuse that power. Within this essay, you will evaluate whether this is an inherently human drive, or if such misconduct regarding those under one's control was ingrained in European culture. For this essay, look for sources delving into the morality of both Europeans and Native peoples.

#3

Along the same lines, you will see a great deal of mistreatment in the chapters coming up, however, that mistreatment led to the spread of the gospel. Was this abuse then worth it? Or did it lead to later generations disavowing Christianity due to previous hardships?

Alternatives to the written assignment:

Scoring of creative projects will be based on time spent and creative integration of themes and concepts from the course. These can be done at a teacher's discretion.

Song/poem — As long as it deals with themes or events/figures from the course, this is fine. Must be full-length song (3–5 minutes) or at least one page of poetry. For this project, multiple 1-page response essays will be required detailing the meaning and influences of the piece.

Painting/drawing — Students are encouraged to stretch their imaginations while displaying themes/people/events discussed in the book.

Scrapbook/photo journal — For this project, finding ways to capture elements from the text in everyday life is key. Whether this means a picturesque view of nature, photos taken at museums/Civil War memorials, or a collection of objects from the 18th and 19th century on display, the key is always cohesion of your intent and creativity.

Assignment (Each answer is worth 10 points.)

True / False:

1. The Portuguese were the only other people interested in colonization in the 16th century. T/F

2. France found great success in its colonization pursuits. T/F

3. Ignatius encouraged the preservation of and care for the natural world above all else. T/F

4. The French colonies were focused on fur trading and fishing expeditions. T/F

5. Québec was a successful French settlement that was not friendly with the local native peoples. T/F

Fill in the blanks:

6. In 1663, _____ was just a commercial branch operation.

7. _____ sold Louisiana to the fledgling United States.

8. Man is created to _____, reverence, and serve God our Lord.

9. _____ posited a theory that in order for a nation to be great, it must have colonies to provide natural resources and markets for the home industries.

10. Samuel de Champlain founded the first successful French settlement at Québec in _____.

Assignment (Each answer is worth 10 points.)

True / False:

1. North American migration was an irregularity in human history. T/F

2. European migration differed from Greek migration in that the Greeks retained affection for their homeland. T/F

3. The English hastened to beat the French, Spanish, and Dutch in their colonization efforts. T/F

4. The Powhatan confederacy successfully destroyed Jamestown. T/F

5. Most of the immigrants to America paid their own way. T/F

Fill in the Blank:

6. The tide of _____ that set in toward the shores of North America during the early years of the 17th century was but one phase in the restless and eternal movement of mankind upon the surface of the earth.

7. One of the worst investments in the early 17th century was an investment in the _____ Company.

8. Many of the emigrants were men of wealth, as the old lists show, and all of them, with few exceptions, were men of _____ and good standing.

9. Indentured servants differed from the serfs of the feudal age in that they were not bound to the soil but to the _____.

10. A bondman could not _____ without his master's consent.

Assignment (Each answer is worth 10 points.)

True / False:

1. Virginia had the first African American slaves. T/F

2. Some white Americans used sophisticated terminology to disguise their racism. T/F

3. Human loss was low on slave ships. T/F

4. The African American church was a place of defiance. T/F

5. Many Southerners found slavery morally repugnant. T/F

Fill in the Blank:

6. The institution of slavery had existed in Western Civilization since _____ times.

7. _____ was not institutionalized in America until some white Americans created a language to describe American people groups.

8. A system of _____ arose.

9. Most slaves were taken from the western part of _____.

10. Never, ever did slaves _____, much less gratefully, accept their condition.

Assignment (Each answer is worth 10 points.)

True / False:

1. Hudson was trying to find a shortcut to China and the Indies. T/F

2. The Hudson River had a strong current. T/F

3. Catholics were ordered by law to attend the Church of England. T/F

4. The payment for Maryland was two arrows. T/F

5. Lord Baltimore died in Maryland. T/F

Fill in the Blank:

6. In 1609 Henry Hudson discovered the Hudson _____.

7. Hudson set out from the port of _____ in 1609, in a vessel named the Half Moon.

8. Lord Baltimore was a _____.

9. The native groups and the _____ in Maryland lived and worked together side by side.

10. _____ was the first settlement in America in which all Christian people had entire liberty to worship God in whatever way they thought right.

For this week's assignment, take time reading your sources and gathering quotes. If you chose a creative project, take your course time to work on it.

Assignment (Each answer is worth 10 points.)

True / False:

1. The Church of England was attempting to establish a middle course between Roman Catholicism and the ideas of the Protestant reformers. T/F

2. Jamestown possessed a spiritualism lacking in the Plymouth settlement. T/F

3. The stated purpose of the Pilgrim expedition was to worship God in a place and in a fashion that was more conducive to their worldview. T/F

4. The Pilgrims came to the New World bitter and resentful toward England. T/F

5. The Pilgrims sought to "purify" the Church of England. T/F

Fill in the Blank:

6. These religious _____ believed that the true church was a voluntary company of the faithful under the spiritual direction of a pastor.

7. Captain Myles Standish, with a number of men, explored the surrounding country, stealing Native American _____ buried in the sand.

8. Myles Standish, with the others, went back to the Mayflower with a _____ report.

9. Massasoit was the chief of the _____ Tribe.

10. When the Pilgrims had their first _____, they invited Massasoit and his men to come and share it.

Assignment (Each answer is worth 10 points.)

True / False:

1. Unlike the Pilgrims, the Puritans did not desire to separate themselves from the Church of England. T/F

2. Massachusetts Bay was a democracy. T/F

3. John Eliot was the first governor of Massachusetts Bay. T/F

4. In 1634, the General Court adopted a new plan of representation that became a prototype for American representative democracy. T/F

5. Puritans lived rigid, joyless lives. T/F

Fill in the Blank:

6. Another Puritan who was not welcome in _____ was Roger Williams.

7. Roger Williams upset the elders by denouncing the _____ Bay charter.

8. Williams departed from Massachusetts on his own accord and spent _____ months living with local Native Americans.

9. Williams founded the first _____ church.

10. Williams called for the complete _____ of church and state.

Assignment (Each answer is worth 10 points.)

True / False:

1. King Charles II of England lent a large sum of money to a young Englishman named William Penn. T/F

2. William Penn was given Pennsylvania. T/F

3. James Oglethorpe founded a colony named Georgia in honor of King George II. T/F

4. Oglethorpe belonged to the Society of Friends. T/F

5. Fifty convicted "witches" were hanged around Salem, Massachusetts. T/F

Fill in the founders for each colony listed.

Colony	Founder	Date	Reasons for Settlement
6. Virginia		1607	Profit
7. Plimouth Plantation		1620	Religious Freedom
8. New Hampshire and Maine		1622	Religious Freedom (from Massachusetts)
9. Massachusetts		1630	Religious Freedom
10. Connecticut		1636	Economic Opportunity

Assignment (Each answer is worth 10 points.)

True / False:

1. Historiography is the study of how history is written. T/F

2. The telling of history has remained basically the same since the start of the 20th century. T/F

3. Puritans founded Harvard. T/F

4. Historians argue over whether the Puritans were democratic. T/F

5. Hobbes began his political theory with the argument that nature was negative. T/F

Fill in the Blank:

6. Miller argued that the first generation of _____ was imbued with a deep sense of mission.

7. Eliot Morison argued that the Puritans were intellectual heirs of the _____.

8. Some scholars argue that Descartes is the founding father of modern _____.

9. John Locke developed theories of human _____.

10. To Locke, the mind is a _____ sheet of paper upon which experience is written.

This week, you (regardless of which project you chose) will be writing a half-page summary of what you've researched thus far. This summary should include a list of sources and brief summaries of what you've learned from each source.

Assignment (Each answer is worth 10 points.)

True / False:

1. Colonial women provided only household necessities. T/F

2. Obedience without question was expected of wives. T/F

3. Nothing was expected in return of men. T/F

4. A total of only 147 women came to Virginia between 1620 and 1622. T/F

Fill in the Blank:

5. Roles evolved in colonial America from necessity more than _____.

6. Women tended to be more highly _____ in America than in Europe.

7. The leadership in the family practice of religion in New England was often taken by the _____.

8. Many examples can be found indicating that women were often granted _____ and economic rights.

9. The _____ was an essential component of the nuclear family.

10. Women helped in the _____ during stressful growing seasons.

Assignment (Each answer is worth 10 points.)

True / False:

1. The Great Awakening was not one continuous revival, but several revivals in a variety of locations. T/F

2. Neither the Anglicans or the Puritans in Massachusetts Bay were terribly successful in maintaining, much less increasing, religious fervency among their converts. T/F

3. Authoritarian structures of any sort — be they governmental or ecclesiastical — were widely accepted. T/F

Fill in the Blank:

4. Revival began in New _____.

5. The key test of one's election, Whitefield asserted, was whether one had had an _____ experience of conversion.

6. The compromises of the Half-Way _____ were swept aside, and the notion of the church as a body of saints was reclaimed.

7. In areas that were nominally Anglican, the Great _____ had little impact.

8. Jonathan Edwards preached his effective "_____ in the Hands of an Angry God" sermon in which he used the image of a spider dangling by a web over a hot fire to describe the human predicament.

9. Known as the "Great Itinerant," George _____ had a loud voice, and it is said one conversion occurred three miles from where he was preaching.

10. The First Great Awakening was a _____ event in the lives of the American people.

Assignment (Each answer is worth 10 points.)

True / False:

1. Universities have changed little over the years in their attitudes toward Christians. T/F

2. The American university was built solidly on evangelical principles. T/F

3. An early brochure, published in 1643, stated that the purpose of Harvard University (the oldest American university) was "To advance Learning and perpetuate it to Posterity; dreading to leave an illiterate Ministry to the Churches." T/F

Fill in the Blank:

4. In fact, most of the U.S. universities founded before the 20th century had a strongly _____, usually Protestant Evangelical Christian character.

5. By the 1920s, the American university had stepped completely back from its _____ roots.

6. Early universities had _____ as presidents.

7. The secular American university compromised its "soul" for _____ positivism.

8. The secular university became a sort of academic hothouse for _____.

9. Most American universities are full of _____ coming to grips with their Christianity.

10. People are forced to give up convictions regarding what they believe to be true and right if their views appear remotely _____.

Assignment (Each answer is worth 10 points.)

True / False:

1. Paine believed in unalienable natural rights. T/F

2. Government by kings was introduced by the Israelites. T/F

3. Rousseau was staunchly opposed to the works of Nietzsche. T/F

4. Burke thought of revolutions as abstract and idealistic. T/F

Fill in the Blank:

5. Paine openly advocated _____.

6. "Man was born free, and he is everywhere in _____."

7. "All government, indeed every human benefit and enjoyment, every virtue, and every prudent act, is founded on _____ and barter."

8. Thomas Paine was an _____ man, a loser most of his life, but during the beginning stages of the American Revolution he profoundly affected the cause of liberty.

9. "Man was born free, and he is everywhere in chains" was the way _____ most famous book, *The Social Contract*, began.

10. Burke argued that relations between people were purely artificial and political contracts were established on tradition (e.g., the Word of God) and custom — not on humanistic notions of human _____.

Having established sources and explained them, it is now time to write the first draft of your introductory paragraph and works cited page.

If you chose a creative project, take your course time to work on it.

Assignment (Each answer is worth 10 points.)

True / False:

1. The colonial period was an epoch of migration. T/F

2. The English government gave the colonies great freedom in terms of local government and taxation. T/F

3. Religious brotherhoods banded together and borrowed or furnished the funds necessary to pay the way to America. T/F

4. The language, the law, and the literature of England furnished the basis of social anarchy. T/F

Fill in the Blank:

5. The Pilgrims and Puritans of New England, the French Huguenots, Scotch-Irish and Irish, and the Catholics of Maryland, fled from _____ governments that denied them the right to worship God.

6. Each colony in time developed its own _____ elected by the voters; it grew accustomed to making laws and paying taxes for itself.

7. It was the protection of the British _____ that prevented Holland, Spain, and France from wiping out their settlements.

8. _____ were farmers who owned their own land and tilled it with their own hands.

9. The majority of freeholders were _____ — critics, not friends — of the Church of England.

10. A thousand circumstances had helped to develop on this continent a nation, to inspire it with a passion for _____, and to prepare it for a destiny greater than that of a prosperous dominion of the British Empire.

Assignment (Each answer is worth 10 points.)

True / False:

1. In the beginning of the 18th century, the American Colonies clearly felt a deep connection to England. T/F

2. Minister Townshend, to balance the budget, promised that he would tax the Americans. T/F

3. John Locke argued, there were certainly inalienable rights that even states could not take away. T/F

Fill in the blank:

4. The _____ Acts were passed in 1774 to punish the colonists for the Boston Tea Party.

5. The _____ Act was established on March 24. It required the colonial authorities to provide housing and supplies for the British troops.

6. Jean-Jacques' _____ *The Social Contract* stated that government existed only by consent of the governed.

7. The _____ Acts gave a monopoly of colonial commerce to British ships.

8. The _____ of 1763 mandated that no further settlements would occur west of the Appalachian Mountains.

9. Thomas _____ wrote an influential book titled *Leviathan* in which he detailed the idea of the social contract, which stated that men originally formed governments because of their need for protection.

10. _____ was an economic theory stating that colonies existed solely for the benefit of the mother country.

Assignment (Each answer is worth 10 points.)

True / False:

1. The conflict between England and France in North America centered on the spice trade and control of several key outposts. T/F

2. The Iroquois were perhaps the most politically powerful group of native people in the history of North America. T/F

3. To restore the balance of power in favor of their allies, the English began selling firearms and ammunition in limited numbers to the Huron and Algonquin. T/F

4. The Iroquois formed a bond of fellowship with the French. T/F

Fill in the Blank:

5. An _____ race developed, in which tribes providing the most fur had a military advantage over those that did not.

6. The French and Indian War was part of a world war called the "_____ years' war."

7. The turn of the 18th century was marked by open colonial _____ between France and England.

8. A post constructed at Detroit in 1701 blocked the _____ from the three northwestern lakes.

9. General _____ led an army of British regulars and colonial irregulars to attack Fort Duquesne.

10. In 1758, British General Forbes captured Fort _____ and renamed it Fort Pitt.

Assignment (Each answer is worth 10 points.)

True / False:

1. The downfall of the French was their insistence that the Natives were their enemy. T/F

2. By the time Washington was 16, Lord Fairfax hired him to measure his land for him. T/F

3. George Washington's father died when George was only 11 years old, leaving him, with his brothers and sisters, to the care of their mother. T/F

4. Washington reached the fort and the French commander gladly gifted him and the British all the land. T/F

Fill in the blank:

5. Young Washington learned _____; and could earn five to ten dollars a day doing this.

6. Major Washington dressed himself like a _____ and set out on his journey through what was called the Great Woods.

7. The guide was in the pay of the French, and he intended to _____ Washington in the woods.

8. When Major Washington got back to Virginia, the governor made him _____.

9. The war ended by the English getting possession of the whole of America from the Atlantic Ocean to the _____ River.

10. The King of England wanted the people in the 13 colonies to pay the cost of keeping _____ to protect American interests.

Compose an outline of your paper, being careful to include an intro, body paragraphs, and a concluding paragraph. Each section of the outline should be a sentence long. An outline helps focus your thoughts so that each paragraph (intro, body, and conclusion) is represented by one sentence summarizing what the paragraph will include.

If you chose a creative project, take your course time to work on it.

Assignment (Each answer is worth 10 points.)

True / False:

1. The news of the tea riot in Boston confirmed King George in his conviction that there should be no soft policy in dealing with his American subjects. T/F

2. The Congress disagreed over whether to stop the importation of British goods into America. T/F

3. By hurried and irregular methods, delegates were elected during the summer, and on September 5 the Congress duly assembled in Carpenter's Hall in Philadelphia. T/F

4. The second Continental Congress, which met at Philadelphia in May 1775, was convinced that conciliation was beyond human power. T/F

Fill in the Blank:

5. Parliament passed five harsh measures, known as the five _____ Acts.

6. Just as the representatives of America were about to present the last petition of Congress to the king on August 23, 1775, George III issued a proclamation of _____.

7. General Gage, hearing that _____ stores had been collected at Concord, dispatched a small force to seize them.

8. Although the Congress had not given up all hope of reconciliation in the spring and summer of 1775, it had firmly resolved to _____ American rights by arms if necessary.

9. In the early days of 1776, Thomas Paine issued the first of his famous tracts, "_____ Sense."

10. The way was fully prepared, therefore, when, on June 7, the Virginia delegation in the Congress moved that "these united colonies are and of right ought to be free and independent _____."

Assignment (Each answer is worth 10 points.)

True / False:

1. The American Army — called the Continental army — never contained more than one-tenth of military-age Americans. T/F

2. States had few Tories or Loyalists. T/F

3. America was a land of rural farms and small towns — it was not dependent upon its urban centers. T/F

Fill in the Blank:

4. The war that opened with the battle of Lexington on April 19, 1775, and closed with the surrender of Cornwallis at Yorktown on October 19, 1781, passed through two phases — the _____ phase until 1778 and the southern phase until the end.

5. A mediocre general at best, George _____ managed to lose virtually every battle he fought.

6. On July 2, Congress voted in favor of independence, and on July 4, the _____ of Independence was approved.

7. On December 26, Washington launched a surprise attack against a British fortification at Trenton, New Jersey, that was staffed by _____ soldiers.

8. On June 14, _____ declared that the flag of the United States would consist of 13 alternating red and white stripes, and a blue field with 13 white stars.

9. After a discussion lasting more than a year, the Articles of _____ were adopted by Congress, although the states did not ratify the Articles until 1781.

10. In 1781, key British points were soon held by the Americans and French, and British General _____ soon surrendered, giving up almost 8,000 men.

Assignment (Each answer is worth 10 points.)

True / False:

1. Abigail Adams homeschooled her children. T/F

2. Women commonly participated in formal education. T/F

3. John Adams gave up a life as a lawyer to become a small-town pastor. T/F

4. Abigail Adams was seen as a threat by some men of her day. T/F

5. Adams was a strong supporter of human rights. T/F

Fill in the Blank:

6. Abigail Adams thought a _____ education for children, especially her daughters, was necessary.

7. Abigail Adams was fervently opposed to _____.

8. Abigail Adams said, "Remember all men would be _____ if they could."

9. As the wife of the first vice president, who became the second U.S. president, the First Lady had a great _____ on the many people of the nation.

10. Abigail courageously objected to laws that did not allow equal rights and privileges for _____.

Assignment (Each answer is worth 10 points.)

True / False:

1. Historians agree that the American Revolution was the single most important event in this nation's history. T/F

2. George Bancroft saw the Revolution in shades of moral gray. T/F

3. Arthur Schlesinger argued that the revolution was a struggle between classes, as evidenced by the very large loyalist group. T/F

4. Religion was unanimously disregarded as a cause of the war. T/F

Fill in the Blank:

5. Within 20 years — 1763 to 1783 — Americans declared their independence, waged a successful war, and became a _____.

6. Some historians argue that the _____ became a means by which humbler colonials challenged the prerogatives of their social "betters."

7. Professor Christine Leigh Heyrman views the first Great Awakening, at least in the North, as an essentially _____ movement.

8. Challenges to _____ and class privilege faded quickly in the wake of the War.

9. Some scholars like Harry Stout have argued that the first Great Awakening radically transformed and democratized modes of mass _____.

10. The strongest case for this interpretation in the North has been advanced by Gary Nash in *The Urban* _____, a wide-ranging study of major seaports in the 18th century.

Having created an outline, it is now time to start work on the main body of the essay. Write the introductory paragraph, which should begin with why the topic is significant, then move into your thesis. The thesis should be the driving force of the paper, about one or two sentences long, stating why the reader should care and making an argument for what is presented.

If you chose a creative project, take your course time to work on it.

Assignment (Each answer is worth 10 points.)

True / False:

1. The 13 colonies of America were tentatively held together by a document known as the Articles of Confederation. T/F

2. In the Continental Congress, which consisted of a single legislative chamber, states had votes based on their size. T/F

3. Congress was reviled by American citizens due to its heavy taxes. T/F

4. Many disputes among the states arose, and there was no federal judicial or legislative branch to solve them. T/F

Fill in the Blank:

5. Industry and _____ were benefitting from the expanded markets generated by post-war peace, immigration, and western expansion.

6. In 1786 an armed rebellion called _____ Rebellion broke out in western Massachusetts.

7. Some people were calling for a return to a _____ — much like the British system from which they had departed.

8. _____ predominated among the 55 delegates — the average age was 42.

9. Alexander _____ advocated calling upon all the states to appoint representatives for a meeting to be held the following spring in Philadelphia.

10. The Articles of _____ tentatively held together the 13 colonies of America. Drafted in 1777, the articles established a covenant among the 13 states.

Assignment (Each answer is worth 10 points.)

True / False:

1. In the beginning, there were too few competing interests between states. T/F

2. Generally, the delegates were proponents of the philosopher John Locke, who argued that the government that governed the least, governed the best. T/F

3. The founding fathers firmly believed that there were certain rights that were given to man by God and could be neither modified nor abrogated by man. T/F

4. The House of Representatives was composed of delegates whose number was fixed at one per state. T/F

5. In the autumn of 1788, Washington was more or less appointed by acclamation, because he did not seek the office. T/F

Fill in the Blank:

6. The idea of a balanced government led to the conviction that three equal and separate branches of government should be established: legislative, _____, and judicial.

7. The _____ was to be composed of an equal number of representatives from all the states.

8. By December 1791, enough states had ratified 10 amendments to make them part of the Constitution, collectively known as the Bill of _____.

9. The _____ Act, operative for two years only, gave the president the power to expel or imprison aliens in time of war.

10. Bill of Rights: _____ to the constitution to protect personal rights, virtually unanimously voted through.

Assignment (Each answer is worth 10 points.)

True / False:

1. The greatest damage Kant did to Christian thought was his argument that morality began with rational thought. T/F

2. Immanuel Kant argued that our knowledge completely transcends our experience. T/F

3. Voltaire argued persuasively that knowledge is unbound by experience. T/F

4. Along with Rousseau, Voltaire was the father of both the Enlightenment and the French Revolution. T/F

Fill in the blank:

5. My _____ tells me that God exists: but it also tells me that I cannot know what He is. (Voltaire)

6. Act as if the maxim of your _____ were to become through your will a general natural law. (Kant)

7. I see then, with regret, that all that has been written about the _____ teaches us nothing at all. (Voltaire)

8. It seems clear to me that God designed us to live in _____ — just as He has given the bees the instincts and the powers to make honey. (Voltaire)

9. All _____, then, will not have the same laws, but no society will be without laws. (Voltaire)

10. To be beneficent when we can is a _____. (Kant)

Assignment (Each answer is worth 10 points.)

True / False:

1. From the end of the Constitutional Convention to the American Civil War, most arguments were conceptualized in discussions about personal rights and exportation laws. T/F

2. Lawyers have argued for two centuries about what the framers intended. T/F

Fill in the Blank:

3. The _____ remains one of the most controversial documents in American history.

4. Greater controversy is tied to the _____ of the original framers of the Constitution.

5. The _____ school subscribed to the idea that the orderly progress of civilization was due largely to the ability of America to provide leadership to the entire world.

6. _____ saw the Constitution as a radical break from the Revolution.

7. _____ argued that the Constitution was more of a consensus than a break from the past.

8. New _____ argued that the Constitution was not an American document at all.

9. New _____ historians argue that the Constitution was a radical departure from European history and a veiled attempt to control Americans and to bring a form of tyranny.

10. After the Civil War, _____ distinct theories arose concerning the Constitution.

Begin composing the body paragraphs. As you do so, try to write efficiently instead of getting bogged down in the details, as certain Fridays will be dedicated to revision. Body paragraphs build off of the thesis, each one being self-contained while still being interconnected.

If you chose a creative project, take your course time to work on it.

Assignment (Each answer is worth 10 points.)

True / False:

1. In 1800, for the first time in history, a democratically elected government peacefully replaced an entirely different ideological government. T/F

2. President Adams, praised for the popular Alien and Sedition laws, made for a close campaign. T/F

3. Had it not been for vigorous opposition by Alexander Hamilton, Thomas Jefferson would have been the third president of the United States. T/F

4. Believing America to be a haven for the oppressed, Jefferson urged a liberal naturalization law. T/F

Fill in the Blank:

5. As a wave of Jeffersonian fervor swept the nation, state after state abolished property qualifications for the ballot and passed more humane laws for debtors and _____.

6. Jefferson pursued a policy of expansion, seizing the opportunity when Napoleon Bonaparte offered to sell the Louisiana Territory for pennies an acre, which was called the Louisiana _____.

7. Jefferson sent Meriwether Lewis and William Clark on an expedition of _____ across the continent.

8. Aaron Burr, who had been elected Jefferson's vice president in 1800 but was replaced in 1804, led several western conspiracies, and killed Alexander Hamilton in a _____.

9. In the case of Marbury v. Madison in _____, the Supreme Court first exercised the power of judicial review.

10. _____ presidency was dominated by foreign affairs, and war was declared in June 1812.

Assignment (Each answer is worth 10 points.)

Fill in the Blank:

1. Internally, the decisions of the Supreme Court under Chief Justice John Marshall promoted _____ by strengthening Congress and national power at the expense of the states.

2. The real changes in America from 1800 to 1828 were in the _____ realm.

3. The concern over whether or not the federal government would pay for public projects was answered tentatively by the federal government's support of the _____ Road.

4. Efficient transportation naturally had a positive effect on _____.

5. While the country grew closer together by more efficient _____, it grew further apart ideologically and politically.

Words to Know (important concepts taught in the course):

6. The _____ Doctrine (1823): declared that the United States would not become involved in European affairs and would not accept European interference in the Americas.

7. John Quincy Adams: an intelligent, principled man, saw his presidency sabotaged by _____ Democrats.

8. The Missouri _____ (1820): tried to answer the problem of slavery expansion by stating that slavery was to be confined to the area south of the Missouri border.

9. The _____ Canal: the most successful private project constructed during the era, enabled efficient western grain producers to ship their produce east and therefore encouraged western expansion.

10. Era of Good _____: a nationalist and industrial period of time during which unity prevailed. Occurred between presidents Monroe and Adams.

Assignment (Each answer is worth 10 points.)

Fill in the Blank:

1. John Quincy _____ was a history maker because he refused to give up, even when the nation and some friends rejected him.

2. In 1830, Adams' home state of Massachusetts sent him to the House of _____.

3. Adams was a tireless supporter of _____ rights.

4. In 1836, Southern Congressmen passed a "gag rule" providing that the House automatically table petitions against _____, and Adams tirelessly fought the rule.

5. In 1848, Adams collapsed on the floor of the House from a _____ and was carried to the Speaker's Room, where two days later he died.

Short Answer is worth 50 points:

Recall a person from your life that exhibited characteristics similar to John Quincy Adams in 5 to 7 sentences.

Assignment (Each answer is worth 10 points.)

True / False:

1. Historians have long been impressed by the formative influences that the National Period brought on American history. T/F

2. It was a period of good-feeling peaceful politics. T/F

3. The earliest historians viewed this Era of Good Feeling as the last time of basic unanimity before the nation embarked on the long road to civil war. T/F

4. Throughout most of the 19th century the majority of American historians who wrote about the National Period more or less summed it up as a vicious conflict between Jeffersonian Democrats and Hamiltonian Federalists. T/F

5. With the rise of totalitarian regimes in Europe, Hamiltonian Federalism was a cause for which one could fight and die. T/F

Short Answer is worth 50 points:

As a historian, what do you believe is vital to communicating the truth of historic events and people?

Continue work on body paragraphs and revise your intro. As you do so, look carefully at your thesis. Is it succinct? Can you argue for the truth in it?

If you chose a creative project, take your course time to work on it.

Assignment (Each answer is worth 10 points.)

True / False:

1. Thoreau was a frustrated pastor who gave up his faith and embraced Transcendentalism. T/F

2. To Emerson, the subjective, the emotional, the feelings were the epicenter of human existence. T/F

3. The Enlightenment epitomized the values of logic, certainty, and consistency. T/F

4. The Romantic reveled in facts and certainty. T/F

Fill in the Blank:

5. Writer, philosopher, and naturalist Henry David _____ was a bona fide eccentric who has been the champion of advocates of nonviolence for at least three generations.

6. Thoreau was not harmless: he advanced the heresy called _____.

7. The problem with Emerson and Thoreau was that they were not merely writers — they were _____, philosophers.

Match the quotes to Thoreau or Emerson.

8. The progress from an absolute to a limited monarchy, from a limited monarchy to a democracy, is a progress toward a true respect for the individual. _____

9. There will never be a really free and enlightened State until the State comes to recognize the individual as a higher and independent power. _____

10. We are born believing. A man bears beliefs, as a tree bears apples. _____

Assignment (Each answer is worth 10 points.)

Fill in the Blank:

1. The president was elected by the _____ college chosen by state legislatures, not by direct voters.

2. The Founding Fathers knew there would be "factions" and special interest groups, but they never planned for or expected to see permanent political _____ emerge.

3. In his Farewell Address, President Washington expressed great _____ about the development of political parties.

4–10. Fill in the blanks (each row worth 10 points):

Date	Hamiltonians	Jeffersonians
1791		
1824		
1829		
1834		
1840		
1854		
Present		

Assignment (Each answer is worth 10 points.)

True / False:

1. It wasn't until long after the Civil War that the United States chartered a national banking system. T/F

2. In 1828, the Georgia legislature outlawed the Cherokee government and confiscated tribal lands. T/F

3. Most of the tribe was driven west some 800 miles in a forced march that became known as the Trail of Tears. T/F

4. The most important of the nativist organizations that sprang up in this period was a secret society, the Order of the Star-Spangled Banner, swiftly labeled the "Know-Nothings." T/F

Fill in the Blank:

5. A number of South Carolina citizens endorsed the states' rights principle of "_____," which was enunciated by John C. Calhoun.

6. Ironically, Northerners first suggested _____ the Union.

7. Opponents claimed the bank possessed a virtual _____ over the country's credit and currency, and that it represented the interests of the wealthy few.

8. Andrew Jackson drew his support from the small _____ of the West, and the workers, artisans, and small merchants of the East, who sought to use their vote to resist the rising commercial and manufacturing interests associated with the industrial revolution.

Words to Know:

9. The Ordinance of _____: declared both the tariffs of 1828 and 1832 null and void within state borders.

10. The _____ bank: functioned as the caretaker of federal assets, much as our Federal Reserve System today.

Assignment (Each answer is worth 10 points.)

True / False:

1. Daniel Webster — statesman, lawyer, and orator — was his era's foremost advocate of American Unification. T/F

2. After a legal apprenticeship, Webster opened a legal practice in Portsmouth, New Hampshire, in 1807. T/F

3. Webster vigorously advocated for the War of 1812. T/F

4. Webster joined the Hamiltonian Democratic Party. T/F

5. Webster opposed the high-tariff bill of 1828. T/F.

Fill in the Blank:

6. Webster became a champion of American nationalism, and his words "Liberty and _____, now and forever, one and inseparable!" won wide acclaim.

7. The _____ of Texas in 1845 and the resulting popular war with Mexico, both opposed by Webster, forced the country to face the issue of the expansion of slavery.

8. The election of Andrew Jackson represented the ultimate triumph of American _____.

9. Historians like James Parton argued that Jackson was a despot who introduced awful things such as the _____ system to the American political system.

10. Later historians argued that Jackson was merely an instrument of another elite: Southern _____ interests.

Spend the next two Fridays finishing up the first draft of your body paragraphs.

If you chose a creative project, take your course time to work on it.

Take your first quarterly exam.

Assignment (Each answer is worth 10 points.)

True / False:

1. The election of Andrew Jackson heralded a new phase of American optimism that argued strenuously for Lockian basic rights. T/F

2. Lockian rights excluded minorities, women, the poor, criminals, and organized laborers. T/F

3. Unbridled optimism led to increased voting rights. T/F

4. Women's rights, abolition, public education, and temperance all were part of this great surge of civil faith in the American experiment. T/F

Fill in the Blank:

5. An influential social movement that emerged during this period was the _____ movement, which consisted of opposing the sale and use of alcohol.

6. The _____ Temperance Union called for the renunciation of all alcoholic beverages, and pressed state legislatures to ban their production and sale.

7. Efforts were made to turn mentally challenged asylums and prisons, which stressed punishment, into _____, where the guilty and infirmed would undergo rehabilitation.

8. For the first time in prison history, the use of imprisonment through _____ confinement as the usual method of stopping crime was permanently established.

9. The idea behind solitary confinement was that a person, if isolated from others, would ultimately choose the _____ course of action.

10. The Auburn model influenced the emergence of reform schools and workhouses in the 1820s, such as the New York House of _____ in 1825 that separated juveniles from the adult prisoners.

Assignment (Each answer is worth 10 points.)

True / False:

1. After winning improvements in Massachusetts, Dorothea took her campaign to the South. T/F

2. Women were not allowed to vote, and their education in the 17th and 18th centuries had expanded vastly beyond what it was in earlier centuries. T/F

3. The economic transformation of Northern society from exclusively agrarian interests to a growing industrial base took men away from the home and elevated women to leadership in the home. T/F

Fill in the Blank:

4. In 1848, Cady _____ and Lucretia Mott organized a women's rights convention — the first in the history of the world — at Seneca Falls, New York.

5. Between 1840 and 1850, Americans founded 40 _____ communities.

6. Early attempts at perfection were founded on the notion that mankind could be perfect if it lived in a _____ — not competitive — community.

7. One notable attempt to live this life was _____ Farm, an experiment in communal living that was both scandalous and revolutionary.

8. "Our objectives, as you know, are to insure a more natural union between intellectual and manual labor than now exists; to combine the thinker and the _____, as far as possible, in the same individual." (Ripley)

Words to Know:

9. Dorothea _____: led a struggle to improve conditions for mentally challenged persons who were confined in deplorable conditions.

10. Frances _____: a Scottish lecturer and journalist, publicly promoted women's rights throughout the United States during the 1820s.

Assignment (Each answer is worth 10 points.)

Fill in the blank:

1. Dorothea Dix was a _____ in Boston when she observed the mistreatment of a group of mentally challenged people in an 1841 jail.

2. Dix devoted herself to a _____ to the mentally challenged throughout the United States.

3. "I come to place before the legislature of Massachusetts the condition of the miserable, the desolate, the _____."

4. May you exercise that "wisdom which is the breath of the power of _____."

5. The bill Dorothea Dix was urging on Congress proposed that 10,000,000 acres of land be distributed to each of the states as _____ for the care of the mentally challenged.

6. Under this plan, each state would receive _____ acres.

7. The influence of Dix with congressional leaders led the body to give her an office in the Capitol from which she could _____ for her bill.

8. The bill completed its passage through _____ on March 9, 1854.

9. After months of delay, President Pierce vetoed the bill, justifying his action with an extended argument about the nature and extent of _____ power.

10. The message was an important statement of public policy — and set forth guidelines for the federal role as a _____ agent until well into the 20th century.

Assignment (Each answer is worth 10 points.)

True / False:

1. Charles Fourier was a French existential writer, who believed violent revolution was often the only way. T/F

2. Fourier spent a lot of time developing social theory; i.e., the way people live and work together in an efficacious way. T/F

3. Fourier believed people couldn't live together in a state of nature and that humankind was corrupt. T/F

4. Charles Fourier claimed the concept of the phalanges and communities were deduced from rational planning, and were destined to succeed. T/F

5. Soren Kierkegaard was raised in a Christian family and confessed Christ as his Savior. T/F

Fill in the Blank:

6. "By 'truth' I always understand '_____ truth.' "

7. "The crowd is _____."

8. "To honor every individual human being, unconditionally every human being, that is the truth and _____ of God and love of 'the neighbor.' "

9. "If everyone in truth loved the neighbor as himself, then would perfect human _____ be unconditionally attained."

10. "But never have I read in the Holy Scriptures this command: You shall love the _____."

Final week of working on first draft of body paragraphs. Focus on getting the basics done for this first run through.

If you chose a creative project, take your course time to work on it.

Assignment (Each answer is worth 10 points.)

True / False:

1. In 1789, slavery was legal and practiced almost everywhere in the United States, which wouldn't change until the Civil War. T/F

2. By 1810, the free black population had swelled to 186,446, but slavery too continued to flourish and spread westward. T/F

3. Slavery grew stronger as the invention of the cotton gin and a booming Southern economy made slavery very profitable. T/F

4. William Lloyd Garrison founded in Boston his anti-slavery paper, *The Liberator*. T/F

Fill in the Blank:

5. By 1810, the slave trade to the United States had come to an end and the _____ population began to increase naturally, giving rise to an increasingly large native-born population of African Americans.

6. In the Southern states beginning in the 1770s, increasing numbers of slaves converted to _____ faiths.

7. Many white owners and clergy insisted on slave attendance at _____ churches, since they were fearful that if slaves were allowed to worship independently they would ultimately desire freedom.

8. Through signals, passwords, and messages not discernible to whites, African Americans called believers to "hush _____" where they freely mixed African rhythms, singing, and beliefs with evangelical Christianity.

9. Although there was some hope immediately after the Revolution that the ideals of independence and equality would extend to African Americans, this hope died with the invention of the cotton _____ by Eli Whitney in 1793.

10. _____ became a hugely profitable crop, transforming the Southern economy and changing the dynamics of slavery.

Assignment (Each answer is worth 10 points.)

True / False:

1. Harriet Tubman was an African American who fled slavery and then guided runaway slaves to freedom in the North for more than a decade before the Civil War. T/F

2. She married John Tubman, a black slave from Virginia. T/F

Fill in the Blank:

3. Ultimately, Harriet Tubman joined the militant _____ cause and worked hard to end slavery.

4. Over a period of 10 years Tubman made an estimated 19 expeditions into the South and personally escorted about _____ slaves to the North.

5. The godly Tubman came to be known as "_____."

Short Answer is worth 50 points:

In 5 to 7 sentences, argue for or against Tubman's actions, breaking the law to do what she thought was right. Would you ever do this?

Assignment (Each answer is worth 10 points.)

True / False:

1. Some historians argued that slavery victimized planters and slaves alike. T/F

2. All historians agree that slavery was a net positive for the South. T/F

3. Many 1940s historians argued that slaves resisted slavery at all times, in every way, that they never willingly accepted, much less liked, their subservient role. T/F

Fill in the Blank:

4. The existence of _____ in American culture had a profound and indelible impact on American history.

5. "Paradoxically," a historian wrote, "a people who prided themselves on having created one of the freest societies in the world also sanctioned slavery — an institution that many other nations less free had long _____."

Short Answer is worth 50 points:

In 3 to 5 sentences, debate whether slavery was a negative for the South that brought down slave owners almost as much as slaves, or a net positive that brought great wealth to the South.

Assignment (Each answer is worth 10 points.)

True / False:

1. Frederick Douglass was born in slavery near Mississippi. T/F

2. As a house servant, he learned to read and write with the assistance of his master's daughter. T/F

3. He was such an impressive orator that numerous persons doubted if he had ever been a slave, so he wrote *Narrative of the Life of Frederick Douglass*. T/F

Fill in the Blank:

4. "The Christianity of _____ is a Christianity, of whose votaries it may be as truly said, as it was of the ancient scribes and Pharisees '. . . All their works they do for to be seen of men.' "

5. "Dark and terrible as is this picture, I hold it to be strictly true of the overwhelming mass of professed _____ in America. They strain at a gnat, and swallow a camel."

6. "They attend with Pharisaical strictness to the outward forms of religion, and at the same time neglect the weightier matters of the law, judgment, mercy, and _____."

7. "They love the heathen on the other side of the globe. They can pray for him, pay money to have the Bible put into his hand, and missionaries to instruct him; while they despise and totally neglect the _____ at their own doors."

Short Answer is worth 30 points:

Do you believe that American Christianity has changed since the time of Douglass? Has it gotten better? Worse?

Today will be devoted to revising the body paragraphs. Look for grammatical errors, but especially focus on carrying the thesis throughout the entire paper. Does each body paragraph support the thesis?

If you chose a creative project, take your course time to work on it.

Assignment (Each answer is worth 10 points.)

True / False:

1. Religious history is superfluous to American history. T/F

2. Begun in 1800, the Second Great Awakening was at its peak in the early 1830s. T/F

3. The phrase "religious revival" was originally coined in the 18th century to describe a new phenomenon in which churches experienced an unexpected "awakening." T/F

4. The Awakening grew in the fragile air of pluralism. T/F

5. Pluralism was an unabashed success for religious America. T/F

Fill in the Blank:

6. Alexis de Tocqueville, in his important book _____ *in America* (1834), wrote, "The religious atmosphere of the country was the first thing that struck me on arrival in the United States."

7. Some have sought to make revivalism a purely American and even a predominantly _____ phenomenon.

8. Historian Geoff Waugh writes, "Revival must of necessity make an impact on the _____ and this is one means by which we may distinguish it from the more usual operations of the Holy Spirit."

Words to Know:

9. An _____: a revivalist period in American history that is of significant duration and effect. In England the recognized leader of the "Evangelical Revival" was John Wesley, founder of Methodism and close friend of Whitefield.

10. _____: according to historian M.E. Dieter, is "the movement within the Christian tradition which emphasizes the appeal of religion to the emotional and affectional nature of individuals as well as to their intellectual and rational nature."

Assignment (Each answer is worth 10 points.)

True / False:

1. Camp meetings remained evangelistic outreaches to the unchurched. T/F

2. Physical phenomena have always existed in some measure in popular revival movements. T/F

3. The most famous early 19th-century revivalist was Charles Grandison Finney. T/F

4. Dwight L. Moody, like Finney, kept revivalism in the country away from the powerful social movements that needed its grace. T/F

Fill in the Blank:

5. The public nature of the _____ experience was focused by the introduction of the anxious bench, forerunner of the altar call, by which the serious seeker made his intentions public.

6. Evangelical Christians became the great _____ reformers of the 19th and early-20th centuries.

7. The change of national mood resulting from the economic upheavals that followed World War I, the persistent attacks of such social critics as H.L. Mencken, and the turn toward a gospel of social concern among the larger denominations led to a decline in the influence of _____ in the churches and in American life.

8. Billy Graham's success in working with a broad spectrum of Protestant churches as well as significant segments of _____ radically changed the direction of American revivalism.

9. Graham was an outspoken supporter of _____ equality and social justice.

10. Three major _____ have occurred in American history: the First Great Awakening, the Second Great Awakening, and the Billy Graham Revivals.

Assignment (Essay answer is worth 100 points.)

Essay: Summarize the account of Mrs. Frances Trollope.

Assignment (Each answer is worth 10 points.)

True / False:

1. Charles Finney, a lawyer turned Presbyterian preacher, literally converted thousands of people to the faith. T/F

2. He would enter a town and scores of bars and other unsavory establishments would close. T/F

3. Originally, the human race was put on the foundation of law for salvation. T/F

4. Abel was the natural head of the race. T/F

5. If Adam had continued in obedience forever, sin would still have entered the world through his descendants. T/F

Fill in the Blank:

6. By one man's disobedience many were made _____.

7. When Adam had fallen, there was not the least hope, by the _____, of saving any of mankind.

8. Then was revealed THE PLAN, which had been provided in the counsels of eternity, on foresight of this event, for saving mankind by a proceeding of mere _____.

9. On this covenant of _____ was founded the covenant of grace.

10. The church, as a body, has never yet understood the fullness and richness of this covenant, and that all there is in Christ is made over to us in the _____ of grace.

Finish editing the body paragraphs. As you do so, pay special attention to the content. Is it coherent? Persuasive? Unified in its intention?

If you chose a creative project, take your course time to work on it.

Assignment (Each answer is worth 10 points.)

True / False:

1. The North and the South were always unified, which made the Civil War a massive shock. T/F

2. The combination of an expanding economy, a flood of immigrants, the Second Great Awakening, Manifest Destiny, and the failure of the American political system brought the young republic to the brink of Civil War. T/F

3. The Civil War was a struggle between conflicting worldviews. T/F

Fill in the Blank:

4. Mary Chestnut wrote as the Civil War was beginning to unfold, "We [the North and the South] are _____ because we have hated each other so!"

5. They disagreed over the power of the federal government; they disagreed over tariffs; they especially disagreed over _____ and its expansion westward.

6. The cotton gin more than anything else made cotton a _____ business and assured its future in the Southern economy.

7. Eli _____ supplied the technology for cotton to be king, and the industrial revolution supplied the market.

8. Cotton mills began production in Massachusetts, with _____-powered machinery.

9. In 1828, Congress raised the tariff on imports, in order to protect native industry struggling to compete with _____ manufacturers.

10. Until the invention of the cotton gin, the North and the South were primarily _____ communities.

Assignment (Each answer is worth 10 points.)

True / False:

1. Another change that provoked the Civil War was immigration. T/F

2. The immigrants moved the United States population up from 4 million to 32 million in just 90 years. T/F

3. That bad feelings grew among some Americans toward immigrants came to be called Isolationism. T/F

4. Harriet Beecher Stowe's *Uncle Tom's Cabin* helped unify the country. T/F

5. In the antebellum South, racism and the gospel of prosperity were at constant odds with each other. T/F

Fill in the Blank:

6. To the average, hard-working Protestant American, the _____ pouring into the cities and following the railroads westward spoke unfamiliar languages, wore dissimilar clothes, drank alcohol freely in the grogshops, and increased crime and pauperism.

7. The presence of slavery, as controversial as it might be, as divisive as it may be, in no way assured that the United States would fight a civil war just as it did not cause a civil war in

    _____.

8. The _____ of slavery into new, free territories was a fiery issue.

9. Lincoln changed later, but initially he, like the Republican Party, was _____ to slavery expansion, not to slavery.

10. By 1860, more Americans than ever had _____ relationships with their God and wished to make personal decisions about where they lived and what they owned.

Assignment (Each answer is worth 10 points.)

True / False:

1. "Manifest Destiny" was coined by John L. O'Sullivan, editor of the *Democratic Review*. T/F

2. This idea of destiny allowed Americans to peacefully live their lives on the East Coast. T/F

3. The North predominantly supported the Mexican war. T/F

4. Expansionism ran into problems when the nation discussed whether new states would be slave or free. T/F

5. The Missouri Compromise occurred when Congress took charge of the question of slavery in the territories by declaring it illegal in the huge region acquired by the Louisiana Purchase. T/F

Fill in the Blank:

6. In 1848, northern dissatisfaction with the existing parties formed a new party — the _____ Party.

7. A new Fugitive Slave Law was passed in 1850 that enraged _____ because slave owners could cross into the North and claim runaway slaves.

8. In 1860, the political system became dysfunctional and all _____ was lost.

9. In 1859, John Brown led a raid on the federal arsenal at Harpers Ferry, Virginia, hoping to encourage a _____ uprise.

10. All the different causes that led up to the American Civil War, the expanding of the economy, a flood of immigrants, the Second Great Awakening, Manifest _____, and the rise of Nativism — doomed the Republic.

Assignment (Each answer is worth 10 points.)

True / False:

1. Arthur Schopenhauer, often called the philosopher of optimism, rejected Christianity and embraced atheism. T/F

2. Schopenhauer was a disciple of Immanual Kant who argued that knowledge was separate from experience. T/F

3. Schopenhauer, with both a Romantic and Modern impulse, invited mankind to an arduous task: understanding experience separate from any outside force or reality. T/F

4. Schopenhauer believed that the will is the being-in-itself of everything in the world. T/F

5. For Schopenhauer, happiness is positive, as it allows for the vigor to do what must be done. T/F

Fill in the Blank:

6. For the first time in several hundred years, the philosopher William Godwin spoke seriously about a _____.

7. Godwin wanted to create a society with no _____ or government at all.

8. Subjective goodness and _____ must supersede law and government.

9. The real or supposed rights of man are of two kinds, active and _____. (Godwin)

10. "Morality is nothing else but that system which teaches us to _____, upon all occasions, to the extent our power, to the well-being and happiness of every intellectual and sensitive existence." (Godwin)

Write the first draft of your conclusion, your final paragraph. As you write, remember to summarize your ideas without stating new facts.

If you chose a creative project, take your course time to work on it.

Assignment

Research Day: Take time today to continue writing or researching for your paper.

If you chose a creative project, take your course time to work on it.

Assignment (Each answer is worth 10 points.)

True / False:

1. The American Civil War, 1861–1865, killed more Americans than any other war in history. T/F

2. In the deep South there was unanimous dissent toward secession. T/F

3. The states of the South all joined together to form a new country, the Confederacy, whose capital city was Montgomery, Alabama, and whose new president was Jefferson Davis. T/F

4. The population of the South was similar to that of the North. T/F

Fill in the Blank:

5. "We just want to be left _____," Jefferson Davis proclaimed.

6. The crisis at Fort Sumter, on April 12–14, 1861, forced President Lincoln to raise an _____.

7. In March 1863, Lincoln signed the inevitable draft law, the first national _____ in history.

8. The South never received _____ support or recognition.

9. On September 22, 1863, the _____ Proclamation announced that, unless the states in arms returned to the union by January 1, 1863, the fatal blow at their "peculiar institution" would be delivered.

10. Southern territory had to be _____ and Southern armies beaten on their own ground or worn down to exhaustion there.

Assignment (Each answer is worth 10 points.)

True / False:

1. The war settled for all time the long dispute as to the nature of the federal system as the doctrine of state sovereignty was laid to rest. T/F

2. When the war ended, few had been killed though many more had been wounded. T/F

3. The war expanded the authority of the federal government, with the executive branch in particular exercising broader jurisdiction and powers. T/F

4. Economically, the war was hard on the North, and led to it being an agrarian society for several more decades. T/F

5. The American Civil War brought freedom to nearly 4 million African Americans. T/F

Fill in the Blank:

6. The _____ Amendment forbade the United States or any state to pay any debts incurred in aid of the Confederacy or in the emancipation of the slaves — plunging into utter bankruptcy the Southern financiers.

7. The Southern planters found themselves excluded from public office and ruled over by their former _____ under the tutelage of Republican leaders.

8. The wreck of the planting system was accompanied by a mighty upswing of Northern industry that discovered it did not need King _____.

9. The _____ Act of 1857 imposed duties so low as to presage a tariff for revenue only.

10. The _____ Act of 1862, which stated that 40 acres of federal Western land was free for the taking, stimulated expansion.

Assignment (Each answer is worth 10 points.)

True / False:

1. It's true that Lincoln kept the Union together, but his skewed moral compass led to discomfort among his constituents. T/F

2. Lincoln was an intensely religious man who advanced Judeo-Christian values in his words and actions. T/F

Fill in the Blank:

3. We have come to dedicate a portion of that field as a _____ resting place for those who here gave their lives that that nation might live.

4. The world will little note, nor long _____ what we say here, but it can never forget what they did here.

5. . . . we here highly resolve that these dead shall not have _____ in vain — that this nation, under God, shall have a new birth of freedom — and that government of the people, by the people, for the people, shall not perish from the earth.

6. One-eighth of the whole population were colored _____, not distributed generally over the Union, but localized in the southern part of it.

7. These slaves constituted a _____ and powerful interest. All knew that this interest was somehow the cause of the war.

8. Government claimed no right to do more than to _____ the territorial enlargement of it.

9. Both read the same _____ and pray to the same God, and each invokes His aid against the other.

10. With malice toward none, with _____ for all, with firmness in the right as God gives us to see the right, let us strive on to finish the work we are in, to bind up the nation's wounds, to care for him who shall have borne the battle and for his widow and his orphan. . . .

Revise the final paragraph, checking to make sure that the main thesis is repeated and no new ideas are added or hinted at. It can be difficult to wrap up a paper, but try to summarize your main points and end with a memorable statement.

If you chose a creative project, take your course time to work on it.

Assignment (Each answer is worth 10 points.)

True / False:

1. By the turn of the century, Lee was condemned in the North and praised in the South. T/F

2. Theodore Roosevelt said that, as a military commander, not even George Washington ranked with Lee. T/F

3. Historian Gamaliel Bradford sought to consider his subjects in terms of their environment. T/F

4. Douglas Southall Freeman saw Lee as a master of strategy who excelled at getting the most from his subordinate commanders and his soldiers. T/F

5. During the first years of the Civil War, most Southerners viewed Stonewall Jackson as the Confederacy's military genius. T/F

Fill in the Blank:

6. "Lee was a _____ man, a fair commander, who had everything in his favor."

7. "He never rose to the grand problem which involved a continent and _____ generations."

8. Lee, Freeman concluded, was one of a small number of people "in whom there is no _____ to be explained, no enigma to be solved. What he seemed he was — a wholly human gentleman."

9. The states of the former Confederacy not only had lost a _____ of young men to war but had become the only part of the United States to experience military occupation.

10. To Lee, duty was not a burden but an _____.

Assignment (Each answer is worth 10 points.)

True / False:

1. The period called Reconstruction was between 1865 and 1877. T/F

2. President Andrew Johnson and then Congress enacted legislation and policies that changed America forever. T/F

3. Northern politicians were disinterested in giving rights to former slaves. T/F

4. Southerners, especially ex-Confederates, hoped to regain some of the wealth and influence that they lost in the Civil War. T/F

5. President Johnson came up with his own Reconstruction policy and implemented it to great success. T/F

Fill in the Blank:

6. By January 1864, _____, Louisiana, and Arkansas offered loyal state governments reinstatement on the basis of Lincoln's Reconstruction Plan.

7. Agreeing with _____ that mass execution for treason was not in order, they did not want key Confederate political or military leaders to emerge as leaders of the post-war South.

8. Radical congressional Republicans wanted Southern states treated more like _____ provinces than wayward children.

9. They wished to ensure that mostly _____ blacks had civil rights, especially the vote.

10. Except for _____, which had accepted the 14th Amendment in 1866, the rest of the Confederacy was divided into five military districts, each governed by a major general.

Assignment (Answer is worth 100 points.)

Research day: Research the Reconstruction and answer the question in 7 to 10 sentences: Do you believe Reconstruction was a success or a failure?

Assignment (Each answer is worth 10 points.)

True / False:

1. Interracial marriage was legalized across the board during the reconstruction. T/F

2. In early American culture, race mixing was a social concern as much as a biological concern for some. T/F

3. Ultimately, a person gains status and identity according to which social group he belongs to. T/F

4. In 1860, one-fourth of the African American population of Charleston, South Carolina, was interracial. T/F

5. In the context of a monogamous, nurturing marriage, people of color were lacking legal equality. T/F

Fill in the Blank:

6. African Americans learned race was a category of exclusion and _____ — both in the society at large and in the Church in particular.

7. When you study the Tower of _____ story (Genesis 11:1–9), you see that God separated languages, not races.

8. Revelation 1:7 and 5:9 can actually serve as a challenge for Christians to develop _____ churches, as these verses show that Christ will be embraced by all — regardless of race or creed.

9. The Bible clearly teaches that there is neither _____ nor Greek in Christ Jesus (Galatians 3:28).

10. If the Church can overcome such biases and _____, we will truly manifest the kingdom of God on the earth, and the Church will grow.

This week will be dedicated to overall revisions of the paper. At this point, look for grammatical errors, while making sure the overall flow of the paper is focused.

If you chose a creative project, review your work and add any final touches.

Assignment (Each answer is worth 10 points.)

True / False:

1. Andrew Johnson was the first president to be impeached and was acquitted in the Senate by just one vote. T/F

2. Johnson was literate from a remarkably young age, being taught by his eldest sibling. T/F

3. Johnson twice committed himself to a course of action that he knew would ruin his political career, but he did it anyway because he thought it was right. T/F

4. President Johnson was harsh on the South, believing that only through "tough love" could the nation be mended. T/F

5. He was indeed a man who was by nature and temperament squarely disposed toward justice and the right, and was a determined warrior for his convictions. T/F

Fill in the Blank:

6. As no state can throw a defense over the crime of treason, the power of _____ is exclusively vested in the executive government of the United States.

7. It is one of the greatest acts on record to have brought _____ people into freedom.

8. President Lincoln issued on December 8, 1863, a proclamation of _____ and reconstruction for those areas of the Confederacy occupied by Union armies.

9. By the end of 1865 every ex-Confederate state except _____ had reestablished civil government.

10. The control of _____ over blacks, however, seemed to be restored, as each of the newly elected state legislatures enacted black codes denying African Americans most of the civil and political rights enjoyed by whites.

Assignment (Each answer is worth 10 points.)

True / False:

1. Thomas Dixon's *The Clansman* presents racial conflict as an epic struggle, with the future of civilization at stake. T/F

2. Dixon personally loudly praised slavery and Klan excesses after Reconstruction ended. T/F

3. He argued that blacks must be denied political equality because it leads to social equality and miscegenation, thus to the destruction of both family and civilized society. T/F

4. Throughout his work, white Southern men are the pillars of family life and society, the repositories of all human goodness. T/F

5. Published in 1879, Albion Tourgee's *A Fool's Errand* was an enormously popular book in its time. T/F

Fill in the Blank:

6. "The true object and purpose of Reconstruction should be . . . to secure a development _____ with that of the North, so as to render the country what it has never been heretofore — a nation." (Tourgee)

7. "I do not believe that those who have looked into each other's faces by the lurid light of battle are the fittest persons to devise and execute such _____." (Tourgee)

8. "You do not seem to appreciate the fact, which all history teaches, that there is no feeling in the human breast more blind and desperate in its manifestations, as the bitter scorn of a long dominant race for one they have held in _____." (Tourgee)

9. "In the South. . . . The ballot and the jury-box were jealously _____ from the intrusion of the poor." (Tourgee)

10. "In the darkest hour of the life of the South, when her wounded people lay helpless amid rags and ashes under the beak and talon of the _____, suddenly from the mists of the mountains appeared a white cloud the size of a man's hand." (Dixon)

Assignment (Each answer is worth 10 points.)

Fill in the Blank:

1. "Dead States cannot restore their _____ 'as it was.' " (Stevens)

2. "Unless the law of nations is a _____ letter, the late war between two acknowledged beligerents severed their original compacts and broke all the ties that bound them together." (Stevens)

3. "Hardly ever was there an expression of hearty attachment to the great republic, or an appeal to the impulses of _____." (Schurz)

4. "_____ was the only means by which they could rid themselves of the Federal soldiers and obtain once more control of their own affairs." (Schurz)

5. "We have turned, or are about to turn, loose four million _____ without a hut to shelter them or a cent in their pockets." (Stevens)

6. "The rapid return to _____ and influence of so many of those who but recently were engaged in a bitter war against the Union, has had one effect which was certainly not originally contemplated by the Government." (Schurz)

Match the quotes to Schurz or Stevens.

7. Treason does, under existing circumstances, not appear odious in the South. _____

8. Each House must judge whether the members presenting themselves from a recognized State possess the requisite qualifications of age, residence, and citizenship; and whether the election and returns are according to law. _____

9. It is obvious from all this that the first duty of Congress is to pass a law declaring the condition of these outside or defunct States. _____

10. There is, as yet, among the Southern people an utter absence of national feeling.

_____

Assignment (Each answer is worth 10 points.)

True / False:

1. Dewey coined the phrase "God is dead." T/F

2. Nietzsche said the only reality is this world of life and death, conflict and change, creation and destruction. T/F

3. Nietzsche took the hopeless vision of Naturalism and Social Darwinism away from its natural conclusion. T/F

4. Nietzsche saw that a world where only power prevailed — a world without Christianity — would inevitably lead to totalitarianism and destruction. T/F

5. The "modern superman" lived without God and without any hope of salvation. T/F

Fill in the Blank:

6. John Dewey's views were known as "_____," which emphasizes action and results.

7. According to Dewey, philosophy wasn't a system of _____ but a practical, empirical method of inquiry.

8. Ethical values described a thing's relationship to its _____.

9. Right and wrong, in other words, were not defined by the Word of God but by _____ and practicality.

10. The hardest thing to attend to is that which is closest to _____, that which is most constant and familiar.

Having finished the paper or creative project, make sure that your sources are cited (any style may be utilized, as long as your teacher can effectively search the sources for the information you used) and then write a page reflecting on the process of writing your paper or creating your project.

Assignment (Each answer is worth 10 points.)

True / False:

1. Cheaper, faster, and safer modes of transportation brought millions to America's shores. T/F

2. An expanding economy needed new workers; an almost limitless countryside needed more farmers. T/F

3. There were countless attempts to stop immigration. T/F

4. Chinese immigration was encouraged well into the 20th century. T/F

5. In 1882, Chinese immigration was limited for the next 5 years. T/F

Fill in the Blank:

6. Immigrants became the _____ for the growing dislocation of urbanization and, during the Great Depression, the challenges of unemployment.

7. Immigrants often chose to remain among their own indigenous groups and resisted _____.

8. Immigrant children usually resisted old cultural _____ — like learning the native language — and this caused tension in immigrant families.

Words to Know:

9. _____: refers to moving from a nation permanently to another nation.

10. _____: is the act or process of moving into another nation with the intention of living there permanently.

Assignment (Each answer is worth 10 points.)

True / False:

1. The United States, before it achieved independence and afterward, had little need for immigrants. T/F

2. Colonial administrators tried to use native labor, with greater or lesser success, and they abetted the escalation of the African slave trade, bringing millions of migrants, against their will, to these New World outposts. T/F

3. Immigration played a key role not only in making America's development possible but also in shaping the basic nature of the society. T/F

4. Few women and men came as indentured servants. T/F

5. The 1820s ushered in the first era of mass migration. T/F

Fill in the Blank:

6. Catholic immigrants to the largely _____ United States, primarily Irish women and men, inspired the nation's first serious bout of nativism.

7. Native-born Americans reacted intensely and negatively to the arrival of Chinese people, leading to the passage of the only piece of U.S. immigration legislation that specifically named a group as the focus of restrictive policy, the Chinese _____ Act of 1882.

8. By the 1890s, many Americans, particularly from the ranks of the well-off, white, _____ _____, considered immigration to pose a serious danger to the nation's health and security.

9. The National _____ Act in 1921 not only restricted the number of immigrants who might enter the United States, but also assigned slots according to quotas based on national origins.

10. By 2000, immigration to the United States had returned to its _____ volume, and the United States once again became a nation formed and transformed by immigrants.

Assignment (Each answer is worth 10 points.)

True / False:

1. Albert Einstein was, to a large degree, the grandfather of the atomic bomb. T/F

2. Einstein was born in Ulm, Germany, but spent most of his life in Austria. T/F

3. In 1919, while still in Germany, Einstein observed the bending of light near the sun at a solar eclipse. This helped him deduce the theory of relativity, $E=MC^2$. T/F

4. Einstein was surprised and horrified when Hitler showed his hand as a genocidal dictator. T/F

5. Roosevelt listened to Einstein and set up the Manhattan Project. T/F

Fill in the Blank:

6. The more a man is imbued with the ordered _____ of all events the firmer become his convictions that there is no room left by the side of this ordered regularity for causes of a different nature. (Einstein)

7. To be sure, the doctrine of a _____ God interfering with natural events could never be refuted, in the real sense, by science. (Einstein)

8. For a doctrine which is to maintain itself not in clear light but only in the _____, will of necessity lose its effect on mankind. (Einstein)

9. I do not share the crusading spirit of the professional _____ whose fervor is mostly due to a painful act of liberation from the fetters of religious indoctrination received in youth. (Einstein)

10. The idea of a personal God is an _____ concept which I am unable to take seriously. (Einstein)

Assignment (Each answer is worth 10 points.)

True / False:

1. Karl Marx had a great influence on G.W. F. Hegel. T/F

2. Hegel created a vast speculative and idealistic philosophy in which truth is found not in the part but in the whole and is not absolute but relative. T/F

3. For Hegel, history is a dynamic succession of novel and creative events, the gradual unfolding of reason. T/F

4. The father of Communism, Hegel invited countless millions to a utopia that never fully materialized. T/F

5. Marx argued that history flows inevitably toward a social revolution, which will result in a society without economic classes. T/F

Fill in the Blank:

6. The history of all hitherto existing society is the history of class _____. (Marx)

7. In the earlier epochs of history, we find almost everywhere a complicated arrangement of society into various orders, a manifold gradation of _____ rank. (Marx)

8. The modern _____ society that has sprouted from the ruins of feudal society has not done away with class antagonisms. (Marx)

9. It has but established new classes, new conditions of _____. (Marx)

10. Society as a whole is more and more splitting up into two great hostile camps, into two great classes directly facing each other: Bourgeoisie and _____. (Marx)

Finish any last touches on the paper and submit it. You should have your intro paragraph stating the thesis, several body paragraphs building on the thesis, a concluding paragraph restating the thesis and bringing the paper to a close, and your works cited page.

If you chose a creative project, wrap up any last-minute changes and submit it.

Assignment (Each answer is worth 10 points.)

True / False:

1. While industrial tycoons were squandering America's wealth, evangelical Christians in the name of Christ were tackling the more difficult urban problems. T/F

2. The Gilded Age took its name from a novel by John Grisham. T/F

3. Before 1861, most Americans were businessmen. T/F

4. In a trust, an aggressive group of business people, called trustees, acquire enough shares in several similar firms to control these companies and thereby control a particular market. T/F

Fill in the Blank:

5. In 1873, a credit scandal and the collapse of the Northern Pacific _____ resulted in a recession from which the country finally recovered four years later.

6. Along with the beginning of the modern American _____ movement and a resurgence of the movement for women's rights, the age saw the implementation of Jim Crow laws.

7. Desire for greatness on the seas, partially spawned by Alfred Thayer Mahan's *The Influence of Sea Power upon History* (1890), led the United States into war with _____ in 1898.

Words to Know:

8. The _____ Act (1862): opened the West for settlement by individual farmers.

9. The _____ Antitrust Act of 1890: declared illegal all strikes that hampered interstate commerce.

10. The Interstate _____ Commission: created in 1887, but its limited powers were further circumscribed by Court decisions.

Assignment (Each answer is worth 10 points.)

True / False:

1. The American laborer began in the Commonwealth of Massachusetts when the first child labor law (1836) was passed, whereby employment of children under the age of 15 was forbidden in incorporated factories. T/F

2. In 1877, a secret miners' association called the Molly Maguires burned buildings and murdered bosses who offended them. T/F

3. As the economy improved over the next few years, American labor stayed its labor course, steadily progressing. T/F

4. Unlike other labor unions, the Knights of Labor encouraged African Americans to join, so that by 1886, approximately 60,000 African Americans had become members. T/F

Fill in the Blank:

5. Laissez-faire policies stated that "the functions of the state should be limited to internal police and foreign _____ — no public education, no limitation of hours of labor, no welfare legislation."

Words to Know:

6. The Order of the _____ of Labor: their goal was to increase negotiating powers by unionizing all American workers.

7. The _____ Contract Labor Law of 1885: prohibited laborers migrating to America who had a contract to perform work.

8. The Massachusetts' _____ Act (1874): adequately enforced woman — and child — labor limits.

9. The New York act of _____: prohibited the manufacture of cigars in sweatshops, but was overturned by the state's highest court.

10. The Sherman _____ Act of 1890: authorized federal action against any "combination in the form of trusts or otherwise, or conspiracy, in restraint of trade," and was used as a blanket injunction against labor.

Assignment (Each answer is worth 10 points.)

True / False:

1. The rise of American industry and immigration labor in the decades following the Civil War was short lived. T/F

2. Industrialization had a fundamental effect on the way Americans saw their world. T/F

3. Traditionally, Americans were accustomed to think in terms of societal values. T/F

4. By the end of the 19th century, it was becoming more difficult to conceive of industrial progress solely in terms of the achievements of a few individuals. T/F

5. This loss of the so-called myth of hard work — that the sky was the limit if one was willing to work hard — was of great concern to late 19th-century Americans. T/F

Fill in the Blank:

6. Vernon L. Parrington wrote that America needed men who stood against the evil _____ who were "cesspools that were poisoning the national household."

7. Many of the participants of these reform movements were _____.

8. John _____ stated that there never were any "good old days."

9. Marxist historians naturally saw history developing along _____ lines, not along ideological lines.

10. Some historians writing in the Great Depression criticized Hicks and Parrington for seeing history as a _____ play where good always triumphed over evil.

Assignment (Each answer is worth 10 points.)

True / False:

1. Vladimir Lenin's worldview never got put into practice. T/F

2. Philosophers talked about the world changing, but Lenin actually brought it about through his actions as well as his words. T/F

3. The Russian Revolution in 1917 amounted to little. T/F

4. Lenin was impatient with Marxist theorizing, which, he believed, had spent too long discussing the perfect state of revolutionary consciousness among the working classes. T/F

5. Lenin did not believe that the working classes would have enough energy and expertise to start a revolution. T/F

Fill in the Blank:

6. The working people would need the help of an "_____" to guide them.

7. Lenin was a Marxist/Hegelian and believed that conflict among classes was both desirable and

   _____.

8. Lenin believed strongly that once the workers' _____ began, it would not stop until it spread all over the world.

9. "I assert: that no movement can be durable without a stable organization of leaders to maintain _____."

10. "The organization must consist chiefly of persons engaged in revolutionary activities as a _____."

Take your second quarterly exam. You may look back over the worksheets from this quarter to help you prepare.

Assignment (Each answer is worth 10 points.)

True / False:

1. Poverty levels at the time were at an all-time low. T/F

2. During this time, the number of people living in cities grew exponentially. T/F

3. This urban growth, to a large degree, was due to the Industrial Revolution. T/F

4. The pietistic, revivalistic, and holiness Christian movements of the latter part of the 19th century were actively involving themselves in evangelical social work that was critical to the lives of thousands of average urban Americans. T/F

5. Revivalist movements like the Salvation Army, the Volunteers of America, the Christian and Missionary Alliance, and the "Rescue Movement" played it safe during the Gilded Age. T/F

Fill in the Blank:

6. But obedience to _____ injunctions to preach the gospel to all people, in the evangelical revivalist mind, also required a profound empathic identity with the poor.

7. In general, mainline Christianity praised _____ and unabashedly used it as a yardstick for spirituality.

8. D.L. Moody never made a general appeal for _____.

9. This was the last era in American history in which most social _____ reform occurred through "nonprofessional volunteers."

10. The Christian social movements were permeated with _____ that affirmed the ministry of women and minorities, transcending cultural barriers of race and class prejudice.

Assignment (Each answer is worth 10 points.)

True / False:

1. Karl Marx was the first philosopher to advance a worldview called anarchy. T/F

2. The philosophy of anarchy argues that all structure — social, political, and religious — is a boon to the development of the human spirit and identity. T/F

3. Proudhon mistrusted all authority. T/F

4. Spencer and other Darwinists loved Proudhon's views — for they suggested that there could be order from chaos — the bedrock of evolutionary social and biological theory. T/F

5. Proudhon invited the world to chaos that was finally realized in the excesses of 1960s America. T/F

Fill in the Blank:

6. "Man is by nature a _____," Proudhon admitted, "that is to say not essentially a wrongdoer but rather wrongly made, and his destiny is perpetually to re-create his idea in himself."

7. From the moral and intellectual point of view, society, or the collective man, is especially distinguished from the individual by spontaneity of action, or _____. (Proudhon)

8. Our society is governed by _____ which, at first blush, exhibit no deliberation and design, but which gradually seem to be directed by a superior power. (Proudhon)

9. The _____ movement was popular in the late 19th-century labor movement in the United States.

10. On May 3, 1886, a strike and mass demonstrations broke out at the McCormick Reaper plant in _____.

Assignment (Each answer is worth 10 points.)

True / False:

1. Piled up against the arches, much of the debris in the Johnstown flood massacre caught fire, entrapping forever 80 people who had survived the initial flood wave. T/F

2. The cleanup operation took a few days, as most of the debris washed away. T/F

3. In the aftermath, most survivors laid the blame for the dam's failure squarely at the feet of the members of the South Fork Fishing and Hunting Club, a resort for business tycoons. T/F

4. The South Fork Fishing and Hunting Club tried repairing the dam, and warned people when it wasn't finished; however, no one listened. T/F

5. Members were wealthy Pittsburgh steel and coal industrialists. T/F

Fill in the Blank:

6. On May 31, 1889, Johnstown, Pennsylvania, was devastated by the worst _____ in American history.

7. Johnstown began to prosper with the building of the Pennsylvania Mainline _____ in 1834 and the arrival of the Pennsylvania Railroad and the Cambria Iron Company in the 1850s.

8. By the end of the Civil War, Johnstown was the largest producer of rolling _____ in the world.

9. Because the growing city had _____ the river banks to gain building space, the heavy annual rains had caused increased flooding in recent years.

10. The _____ South Fork Dam had finally broken, sending 20 million tons of water crashing down the narrow valley.

Assignment (Each answer is worth 10 points.)

True / False:

1. Bryan was a strict Darwinist, opposed to any and all religion. T/F

2. Despite a long and distinguished political career, William Jennings Bryan is best known for the decisive defeats that he endured. T/F

3. He was nominated three times to represent the Republican party as their presidential candidate. T/F

4. Bryan led the prosecution of John T. Scopes, a young biology teacher charged with breaking Tennessee law by teaching Darwin's theory of evolution. T/F

Fill in the Blank:

5. "My friends, we declare that this nation is able to legislate for its own people on every question, without waiting for the aid or consent of any other _____ on earth." (Bryan)

6. "When they are confronted with the proposition, they will declare that this nation is not able to attend to its own _____." (Bryan)

7. "Our ancestors, when but three millions in number, had the courage to declare their political _____ of every other nation." (Bryan)

8. "Instead of having a gold _____ because England has, we will restore bimetallism, and then let England have bimetallism because the United States has it." (Bryan)

9. "If they dare to come out in the open field and defend the gold standard as a good thing, we will _____ to the uttermost." (Bryan)

10. "You shall not press down upon the brow of labor a crown of thorns. You shall not crucify mankind upon a cross of _____." (Bryan)

This is the beginning of your next semester-long project, which you will be working on every Friday instead of a traditional lesson/worksheet. Remember, you can select from a range of projects, finding one best suited to your interests. All essays will be five pages or longer and use no less than three chapters from the book, as well as three outside sources. For this first Friday, all that you need to do is select a project and begin gathering the materials required to write it.

Prompts:

#1

A large theme of the second half of the course is the continued march of technology. In what ways do these technological advances help society, and in what ways do they hinder society? Pick three technological advances discussed and research them, making decisions on the overall efficacy of the advances.

#2

Research three of the spiritual leaders discussed in the second half of the book and ascertain what it is about these men and women that allowed them to be vessels for spiritual change. What trends in behavior, background, personality, etc., do you see?

#3

Choose three figures that are inspirational for you and discuss them, being sure to start with brief biographies before launching into why they matter to you.

Alternatives to the written assignment:

Scoring of creative projects will be based on time spent and creative integration of themes and concepts from the course. These can be done at a teacher's discretion.

Song/poem — As long as it deals with themes or events/figures from the course, this is fine. Must be full-length song (3-5 minutes) or at least one page of poetry. For this project, multiple 1-page response essays will be required detailing the meaning and influences of the piece.

Painting/drawing — Students are encouraged to stretch their imaginations while displaying themes/people/events discussed in the book.

Scrapbook/photo journal — For this project, finding ways to capture elements from the text in everyday life is key. Whether this means a picturesque view of nature, photos taken at museums/Civil War memorials, or a collection of objects from the 18th and 19th century on display, the key is always cohesion of your intent and creativity.

Assignment (Each answer is worth 10 points.)

True / False:

1. The Central Pacific was built eastward from northern California, edging over the Sierra Nevada through the efforts of Chinese workers imported for the job. T/F

2. All the major railroads found their financing in different ways. T/F

3. Wherever the railroad went, small towns, industries, and cattle ranches disappeared. T/F

4. Unlike Eastern towns, Western towns could be set up in organized, intentional patterns. T/F

5. One important help for this westward movement was the railroad. T/F

Fill in the Blank:

6. In 1893, Frederick Jackson Turner gave an address to the American Historical Association where he stated that the _____ played a large part in the creation of American democracy.

7. Vast open spaces, free or almost free _____, Native Americans, cattle rustlers, desperados — they are all part of the story that we call the Wild West.

8. With the discovery of California _____ in 1849, there was a need to connect California with the Eastern states.

9. In 1862, Congress agreed to lend hundreds of millions of dollars to two corporations — the Central Pacific in the West and the Union Pacific in the East — to construct the _____.

10. With the help of thousands of _____ immigrant laborers, the Union Pacific Railroad was built westward from Omaha, Nebraska.

Assignment (Each answer is worth 10 points.)

True / False:

1. The railroad development and the resulting population growth were a net positive for Natives. T/F

2. The American military employed a systematic form of genocide unparalleled in American history. T/F

3. Dozens of Native American tribes lived in the West, united in a common purpose and at peace with each other. T/F

4. Tribes like the Arapaho and Sioux were hunters who depended on the 13 million buffalo that roamed the Great Plains. T/F

5. In the Pacific Northwest, tribes like the Nez Perce were fishermen. T/F

Fill in the Blank:

6. Native Americans won some high-profile victories, including the defeat of George _____ on Montana's Little Bighorn River in 1876.

7. The _____ Act of 1887 ended reservations and diminished the importance of the tribe/community by giving lands to individual tribal members.

8. In 1934, the Wheeler-_____ Act preserved the remaining reservations, but the damage was done.

9. Perhaps the most famous Native war chief was _____.

10. "I had not been _____, but some of my people had been, and I fought with my tribe; for the soldiers and not the Indians were at fault." (Geronimo)

Assignment (Each answer is worth 10 points.)

True / False:

1. The West, its reality and myth, has played an important role in the formation of the American ethos. T/F

2. The "Wild" West invited social expansion and unification. T/F

3. In 1878, Billy the Kid was capturing headlines across the American West, escaping for good three years later. T/F

4. Billy the Kid was born in a posh Boston household. T/F

5. In Arizona, Billy the Kid cowboyed, perhaps ran with rustlers, and committed his first authenticated killing. T/F

Fill in the Blank:

6. Billy the Kid became notorious for his involvement in a _____, which became known as the Lincoln County War.

7. Some called Jesse _____ America's Robin Hood.

8. James' father, the Rev. Robert James, was a born-again Baptist _____.

9. During the Civil War, Jesse and his brother Frank rode with the _____ Quantrill and participated in many bloody raids.

10. For the next 15 years after the Civil War, the James boys roamed throughout the U.S., robbing trains and banks of their gold, building a _____ that was to live more than a century after Jesse's death.

Assignment (Each answer is worth 10 points.)

True / False:

1. Westward expansion encouraged women to stay at home. T/F

2. As busy as the pioneer Mrs. Willard was, she found time to homeschool Frances, who was a terrific student. T/F

3. In the 1870s, Frances Willard emerged as a national leader within the temperance movement. T/F

4. Through Willard's writings, she introduced thousands of women to other important social concerns: voting rights for women, safer conditions for American workers, world peace, and methods of improving the nation's schools. T/F

Fill in the Blank:

5. "I went to see 'The Sign of the Cross;' and I frankly own it was to me a _____ of what the theatre might do to help humanity to the heights of purity and holiness." (Willard)

6. "I remembered how I went straight to that _____ without looking to the right or left, and though trembling so that I could feel my heart beat as I went forward." (Willard)

7. "The great heart of humanity may find in that union of music, picture, song, and the actual drama of life, passing before it, many of those lessons whereby we are lifted to a _____ plane." (Willard)

8. "Societies will be organized, and parties will divide on the right of men to make and carry deadly weapons, dynamite and other destructive agencies still more powerful, that human ingenuity will yet _____." (Willard)

9. "There will be an army of earnest souls socially ostracized, as we are now, because they believe that the _____ should cease to kill and the sale of meat be placed under the ban of law." (Willard)

10. "There will be a great movement to _____ the people so that they will use neither tea, coffee, nor any of the numerous forms of anodynes and sedatives." (Willard)

For this week, take time reading your sources and gathering quotes. If you chose a creative project, take your course time to work on it this Friday.

Assignment (Each answer is worth 10 points.)

True / False:

1. The Civil War drastically changed the lives of many African Americans. T/F

2. The so-called Great Migration is one of the most powerful images of black resistance to racism. T/F

3. The Great Migration was the greatest transfer of a population group in world history. T/F

4. The Great Migration was primarily caused by the availability of jobs and the hope that racism would be absent or abated. T/F

5. From 1900 to 1955, most blacks moved from Northern cities to Southern agrarian centers. T/F

Fill in the Blank:

6. Martin Luther King Jr., on a visit to an Alabama plantation in 1965, was amazed to meet sharecroppers who had never seen United States _____.

7. _____ is a term that arose in the 20th century to describe the systematic accumulation of poor Americans into sections of urban America.

8. Whether in the Southern countryside or in the Northern city, _____ remained an inescapable demon.

9. Racism mitigated any economic gains that were everywhere available in the _____ society arising in most cities.

10. By 1930, over two-thirds of the African American population was still working in _____ jobs.

Assignment (Each answer is worth 10 points.)

True / False:

1. Booker Taliaferro Washington was the foremost African American educator of the late 19th and early 20th centuries. T/F

2. In 1881, Martin Luther King, Jr. founded Tuskegee Normal and Industrial Institute in Alabama. T/F

Fill in the Blank:

3. "Cast down your _____ where you are" — cast it down in making friends in every manly way of the people of all races by whom we are surrounded.

4. Our greatest danger is that in the great leap from slavery to freedom we may overlook the fact that the masses of us are to live by the _____ of our hands.

5. No _____ can prosper till it learns that there is as much dignity in tilling a field as in writing a poem.

6. Cast down your bucket among these people who have, without _____ and labor wars, tilled your fields, cleared your forests, builded your railroads and cities.

7. It is important and right that all privileges of the law be ours, but it is vastly more important that we be _____ for the exercise of these privileges.

8. The opportunity to earn a dollar in a factory just now is worth infinitely more than the opportunity to spend a dollar in an _____-house.

9. Nothing in thirty years has given us more hope and encouragement, and drawn us so near to you of the white race, as this opportunity offered by the _____.

10. That higher good, that, let us pray God, will come, in a blotting out of sectional differences and racial animosities and suspicions, in a determination to administer absolute _____.

Assignment (Each answer is worth 10 points.)

True / False:

1. Jim Crow Laws were created after the Civil War by Northern states to control African Americans. T/F

2. Between 1882 and 1968, thousands died of lynching, most of them black men and women. T/F

3. From 1882 to 1901, the annual number of lynchings usually exceeded 100. T/F

4. Lynching was almost non-existent by the 20th century. T/F

Match the Jim Crow law to the state that established it, choosing between Florida, Alabama, and Virginia.

5. The schools for white children and the schools for negro children shall be conducted separately.
   _____

6. All passenger stations in this state operated by any motor transportation company shall have separate waiting rooms or space and separate ticket windows for the white and colored races.
   _____

7. Every person . . . operating . . . any public hall, theatre, opera house, motion picture show or any place of public entertainment or public assemblage . . . shall separate the white race and the colored race. _____

8. All marriages between a white person and a negro, or between a white person and a person of negro descent to the fourth generation inclusive, are hereby forever prohibited.
   _____

9. No person or corporation shall require any white female nurse to nurse in wards or rooms in hospitals, either public or private, in which negro men are placed. _____

10. It shall be unlawful to conduct a restaurant or other place for the serving of food in the city, at which white and colored people are served in the same room. _____

Assignment (Each answer is worth 10 points.)

Match the era of historiography to their description, the eras being Paternalism, Transition, Maturation, and Accommodation.

1. This generation of historians sought to make race a secondary issue, if not absent from historical discussions. _____

2. This generation of historians argued that African American slaves were treated poorly in antebellum and Reconstruction America. _____

3. Historians in this era saw African Americans as docile, benevolent wards of American whites. _____

Fill in the Blank:

4. The second period was the period of _____ — 1920s to 1950s — when the attitudes of scholars toward African Americans began to change and racist views were no longer accepted.

5. They argued forcefully that African Americans were then and always had been victims of _____.

6. Historians recognized that African American history was a _____ and needed to be examined separately from white American history.

7. _____: African Americans are perceived as being inferior to whites.

8. _____: African Americans are beginning to be seen separately from white history.

9. _____: African Americans are finally seen as victims of prejudice.

10. _____: African American history is studied separately from white history.

Having established sources and explained them, it is now time to write the first draft of your introductory paragraph and to plan your works cited page.

If you chose a creative project, take your course time to work on it.

Assignment (Each answer is worth 10 points.)

True / False:

1. During the last quarter of the 19th century, the United States emerged as a world power. T/F

2. The United States' industrial and agricultural productivity, large size, growing population, and modern navy gave it a prominence that could not be ignored. T/F

3. There was little debate that an overseas empire was the right course of action for the U.S. T/F

4. The instability in Latin America invited easy conquest from the U.S. T/F

5. The two great needs of mankind are, first, a pure, spiritual Christianity, and second, civil liberty. T/F

Fill in the Blank:

6. When John Hay, Secretary of State, heard that an _____ citizen, Perdicaris, had been seized by Raisuli, a Moroccan bandit, wired his brusque message: "We want Perdicaris alive or Raisuli dead."

7. Survival of the _____ ideas demanded that the best, the strongest, the most capable dominate the weaker.

8. With a naval base in the Pacific, it was patently obvious that a _____ must be built between the Atlantic and the Pacific Ocean.

9. McKinley's first term coincided with a movement away from _____, which advocated staying out of foreign entanglements.

10. _____ or exaggerated journalism, especially in New York newspapers owned by the competing publishers Joseph Pulitzer and William Randolph Hearst, was enormously successful in creating demand for U.S. intervention in Cuba.

Assignment (Each answer is worth 10 points.)

Fill in the Blank:

1. All that this country desires is to see the neighboring countries stable, orderly, and
   _____.

2. If a nation shows that it knows how to act with reasonable efficiency and
   _____ in social and political matters, if it keeps order and pays its
   obligations, it need fear no interference from the United States.

3. In the Western Hemisphere the adherence of the United States to the _____
   Doctrine may lead the United States, however reluctantly, in flagrant cases of such wrongdoing or
   impotence, to the exercise of an international police power.

4. If every country washed by the Caribbean Sea would show the progress in stable and just
   civilization which with the aid of the Platt amendment _____ has shown since
   our troops left the island . . . all question of interference by this nation with their affairs would be at
   an end.

5. While they thus obey the primary laws of civilized society they may rest assured that they will be
   treated by us in a spirit of cordial and helpful _____.

6. We would interfere with them only in the last resort, and then only if it became evident that their
   inability or unwillingness to do justice at home and abroad had _____ the
   rights of the United States.

7. It is a mere truism to say that every nation . . . which desires to maintain its freedom, its
   independence, must ultimately realize that the right of such independence cannot be separated
   from the _____ of making good use of it.

8. In asserting the Monroe Doctrine . . . we have acted in our own interest as well as in the interest of
   _____ at large.

9. There are, however, cases in which, while our own interests are not greatly involved, strong appeal is
   made to our _____.

10. In extreme cases action may be justifiable and _____.

Assignment (Each answer is worth 10 points.)

Fill in the Blank:

1. During the U.S. war in the Philippines between 1899 and 1904, ordinary American soldiers shared the _____ zeal of their commanders and pursued the Filipino "enemy" with brutality and sometimes outright lawlessness.

2. I met one of our company, who told me that the Fourteenth and _____ were driving all before them, and taking no prisoners.

3. I reached the office at 3 p.m., just in time to see a platoon of the Washingtons, with about _____ prisoners, who had been taken before they learned how not to take them.

4. I am not _____, and am always ready to do my duty, but I would like someone to tell me what we are fighting for.

5. I deprecate this war, this slaughter of our own boys and of the _____, because it seems to me that we are doing something that is contrary to our principles in the past.

6. Most of the general officers think it will take _____, and a large force of soldiers, to thoroughly subjugate the natives.

7. There's no use trying to conceal the fact that many of the men over there now, especially the volunteers, are _____, and tired of fighting way off there, with nothing in particular to gain.

8. The soldiers made short work of the whole thing. They _____ every house.

9. They had four prisoners, and didn't know what to do with them. They asked Captain Bishop what to do, and he said: You know the orders, and four _____ fell dead.

10. Our force is too _____, and we cannot spare any more men, and will have to wait for more troops.

Assignment (Each answer is worth 10 points.)

Fill in the Blank:

1. Mr. _____ is not only disposed to see, in the superior vigor of our people, an illustration of his favorite theory of natural selection, but even intimates that the world's history thus far has been simply preparatory for our future.

2. "There is apparently much truth in the belief that the wonderful progress of the United States, as well as the character of the people, are the results of natural _____."

3. The more energetic, restless, and courageous men from all parts of _____ have emigrated during the last ten or twelve generations to that great country, and have there succeeded best.

4. "All other series of events . . . only appear to have purpose and value when viewed in connection with, or rather as subsidiary to, the great stream of _____ emigration to the West."

5. Some Protestant Americans argued that America should conquer these and other Roman Catholic nations so that _____ "truth" could be reasserted.

6. The principles of Gregory VII and Innocent III [these popes asserted Roman-Catholic dominance over all faiths] are still the principles of the _____ Church.

7. Protestants little know what they are doing when they propose to accept the aid of _____ in the work of Sunday exaltation.

8. Rome is aiming to re-establish her power, to recover her lost _____.

9. God's Word has given warning of the impending danger; let this be _____, and the Protestant world will learn what the purposes of Rome really are.

10. Whoever shall believe and obey the word of _____ will thereby incur reproach and persecution.

Compose an outline of your paper, being careful to include an intro, body paragraphs, and a concluding paragraph. Each section of the outline should be a sentence long. An outline helps focus your thoughts so that each paragraph (intro, body, and conclusion) is represented by one sentence summarizing what the paragraph will include.

If you chose a creative project, take your course time to work on it.

Assignment (Each answer is worth 10 points.)

True / False:

1. For the last time, during World War I, the British army recruited its regiments by county and town, but the trend was exaggerated in the Kitchener armies recruited for World War I. T/F

2. Entire groups of friends were killed together during the war. T/F

3. The war was surprisingly low on casualties for its scope. T/F

4. The world was in a population slump, making the war all the more devastating. T/F

5. The industrial revolution had increased productivity and made possible a flourishing military. T/F

Fill in the Blank:

6. In the summer of 1914, a Serbian nationalist — a citizen of the aging _____ Empire — assassinated the Archduke Francis Ferdinand, the heir to the throne of Austria-Hungary.

7. While President Woodrow Wilson promptly proclaimed the _____ of the United States, the large majority of the American people were without doubt on the side of Great Britain and France.

8. The _____, a British steamer, sailed from New York for Liverpool. On May 7, without warning, the ship was struck by two torpedoes and in a few minutes went down by the bow, carrying to death 1,153 persons, including 114 American men, women, and children.

9. "The military masters of _____," Wilson exclaimed, "denied us the right to be neutral."

10. On January 18, 1919, a conference of the _____ and Associated Powers assembled to pronounce judgment upon the German empire and its defeated satellites: Austria, Hungary, Bulgaria, and Turkey.

Assignment (Each answer is worth 10 points.)

True / False:

1. Some historians argue that imperialism manifested because of economics. T/F

2. The navy was disadvantageous for American businesses. T/F

3. Some historians saw imperialism as a fleeting aberration — an opportunity that arose after an unexpectedly quick military victory in the Spanish-American War. T/F

4. Some historians argue that World War I was an extension of imperialist policies. T/F

5. All of the above arguments more or less agree that imperialism grew out of foreign influences. T/F

Fill in the Blank:

6. Was America justified in her domination in the _____ and Latin American countries?

7. Were America's policies a form of _____ or aggression?

8. The debate among historians about American _____ was in reality not merely an interpretation of the past — it was more a vision of what America ought to be.

9. What caused America to suddenly abandon its _____ in the post–Civil War era and to embrace imperialism?

10. Several other historians argued that the emergence of social _____ provided Americans with an intellectual reason to pursue her imperialist aims.

Assignment (Each answer is worth 10 points.)

True / False:

1. After World War I, a postwar boom began that continued unabated until the Cold War. T/F

2. By 1920, industry was focusing on goods and consumables such as silk stockings, washing machines, and cars. T/F

3. Electricity has had as profound an effect on American culture as any technology in modern times. T/F

4. There were 8,000 motor vehicles in 1900 and nearly a million in 1912. T/F

5. Modern technologies, like radio and movies, promoted discipline and sacrifice, ultimately creating a more religious nation. T/F

Fill in the Blank:

6. Americans, then, for the first time, had a national _____ identity as well as a national political identity.

7. In the middle of the 1920s, for the first time in American history, Americans no longer wished to have six or eight children. On the contrary, Americans sought to have two or three children. _____ of life issues were suddenly more important than child-bearing.

8. The former dominance of the home in the child's life was _____. Young people spent less time in the home than their parents who grew up in the 1890s.

9. The lure of the kindergarten to four- and five-year-olds was irresistible. The invention of the high school was even more influential. Athletics, dramatics, and societies all conspired to _____ the American family.

10. Not all cultural advances were bad. Everyone had more _____ time.

Assignment (Each answer is worth 10 points.)

True / False:

1. President Herbert Hoover had been in office for almost four years when the stock market crashed and quickly passed it off onto his successor. T/F

2. The Great Depression destroyed America's confidence in the future. T/F

3. The Great Depression lasted from 1929 to the beginning of America's involvement in World War II. T/F

4. Roosevelt instituted socialism into the capitalist American society. T/F

5. Hoover enacted the Social Security Act, which provided a safety net and retirement income for workers. T/F

Fill in the Blank:

6. The _____ Market Crash of 1929 and bank failures destroyed most of America's liquid income and savings.

7. The _____ rate rose above 25 percent, which meant, of course, even less spending to help alleviate the economic situation.

8. A huge _____ was imposed against European imports that ultimately caused European governments to retaliate by not selling American goods.

9. Drought conditions lowered productivity in the _____.

10. The New Deal convinced most Americans that their government had a moral and legal right to _____ in public and private affairs if the general good of the public demanded it.

Having created an outline, it is now time to start work on the main body of the essay. Write the first paragraph. An introductory paragraph should begin with why the topic is significant, then move into your thesis. The thesis should be the driving force of the paper, about one or two sentences long, stating why the reader should care and making an argument for what is presented.

If you chose a creative project, take your course time to work on it.

Assignment (Each answer is worth 10 points.)

True / False:

1. Billy Sunday was an evangelist and baseball player. T/F

2. Billy often combined a solid gospel message with a traditional lack of patriotism. T/F

3. In Sunday's lifetime, he addressed over 100 million people with the aid of loud speakers, TV, or radio. T/F

4. Sunday gained nationwide recognition for becoming the first player to run the bases in 14 seconds, and set records for stealing bases. T/F

5. Shortly after being "saved" through the outreach of the Pacific Garden Mission in Chicago, Sunday turned down a $400-per-month baseball salary for an $84-per-month ministry position. T/F

Fill in the Blank:

6. Later in life, he was offered $1 million to be in the _____, but again declined in order to continue the evangelistic ministry God had called him to.

7. Throughout his life, he made it a rule to spend the first moments of his day alone with God and God's _____.

8. "I challenge you to show me where the _____ has ever helped business, education, church morals, or anything we hold dear." (Sunday)

9. Some Christian leaders criticized Billy Sunday for putting too much emphasis on social policy (e.g., prohibition) and not putting enough emphasis on the _____ message.

10. Helen Thompson Sunday devoted herself to her family, and to other young evangelists just starting out. One of these young men was a skinny boy from North Carolina. His first name was also Billy. His last name was _____.

Assignment (Each answer is worth 10 points.)

True / False:

1. To his friends, Franklin D. Roosevelt was a genius/innovator who skillfully guided America through some of her darkest days. T/F

2. The New Deal was a movement mired by inequality. T/F

3. Historian Rexford G. Tugwell argued that Roosevelt went too far with his socialist leanings. T/F

4. Henry Steele Commager argued that Roosevelt's policy was really not radical at all — it was in the spirit and ideology of early reform movements. T/F

5. Others argued that it was very much an "American" solution to the problems facing the Great Depression generation. T/F

Fill in the Blank:

6. "The New Deal, and the thinking it engendered," wrote Hofstadter, "represented the triumph of economic emergency and human _____ over inherited notions and inhibitions."

7. To those historians whose view is that America is founded upon an atomistic philosophy . . . the New Deal will always appear as a movement alien and hostile to traditional

    _____.

8. To those scholars who adhere to a corporate philosophy . . . the New Deal becomes a political movement inspired by proper _____.

9. To his enemies, Roosevelt was a _____ who destroyed ingenuity and free enterprise and replaced them with a welfare state.

10. To those historians who maintain that only a radical restructuring of American society could eliminate _____, racism, war, and equality, the New Deal appears as a palliative or sham designed to gloss over fundamental defects.

Assignment (Each answer is worth 10 points.)

True / False:

1. Karl Schmitt was a German theologian, both brilliant and disturbing. T/F

2. The disillusioning effect of World War I only allowed Schmitt to grow closer to God. T/F

3. Schmitt openly advocated an authoritarian regime since he saw it as the only alternative to morality. T/F

4. Simone de Beauvoir did more to influence modern views of women than any other single person. T/F

5. Beauvoir, working from a philosophy called existentialism, argued that women should gain their identity from the Bible. T/F

Fill in the Blank:

6. The Bible, according to de Beauvoir, was a draconian document that effectively made women _____ to male domination.

7. Martin Heidegger supported Idealism, a philosophical school that argued that reality is an entirely cerebral affair, an affair of the _____.

8. Another German philosopher, Heidegger, like Schmitt, joined the _____ Party and openly supported Hitler.

9. Postmodernism is a philosophical movement that opposes those philosophies that it believes are typically modern, i.e., those centered around the European _____.

10. Heideggeer believed that the essence of human being is not consciousness but _____, not theory but praxis — and he underlined the importance of Being and language.

Assignment (Each answer is worth 10 points.)

True / False:

1. Helen Parris Stobaugh was born at the beginning of the 20th century. T/F

2. Her first husband abused her once and she gently forgave him. T/F

3. It was beneath her to file for divorce, but Judge Merritt knew what she wanted — everyone did — so he filed and granted divorce within the week. T/F

4. Her first husband never remarried and suffered in ebullient regret for the rest of his life — for he remained in love with Helen. For penance, he became a United Methodist pastor. T/F

5. She cared deeply for the thoughts and opinions of others. T/F

Fill in the Blank:

6. A fourth generation Methodist, she loved to visit the Presbyterian church because the pastor's wife wore _____ dresses.

7. When she was banished from the country _____, most felt that she was sufficiently castigated.

8. When she married the wealthiest and most eligible _____ in town, they were only too happy to invite her back into the country club.

9. She refused, and all her _____ and generations following grew up as pariahs — without the benefit of Southern country club amenities.

10. Helen Parris Stobaugh allegedly never again set a foot in the Desha County Country Club — although she loved to have garden _____ and social events in her house.

Begin composing the body paragraphs. As you do so, try to write efficiently instead of getting bogged down in the details, as certain Fridays will be dedicated to revision. Body paragraphs build off of the thesis, each one being self-contained while still being interconnected.

If you chose a creative project, take your course time to work on it.

Assignment (Each answer is worth 10 points.)

True / False:

1. Adolf Hitler wanted more land, especially in the east, to expand Germany according to the Nazi policy of lebensraum [territory for political and economic expansion]. T/F

2. Hitler used the harsh limitations that were set against Germany in the Versailles Treaty as reason to stick to one's own land. T/F

3. Germany wasn't allowed to take over both Austria and Czechoslovakia without a fight. T/F

4. To eliminate the possibility of the Soviet Union fighting if Poland were attacked, Hitler made a pact with the Soviet Union — the Nazi-Soviet Non-Aggression Pact. T/F

5. On September 1, 1939, Great Britain and France sent Hitler an ultimatum — withdraw German forces from Poland or Great Britain and France would go to war against Germany. T/F

Fill in the Blank:

6. The outbreak of World War II in Europe proved to be an important turning point in the development of American foreign policy, back to the America of the _____, which now wished to be left alone and out of European politics.

7. On December 7, 1941, America was attacked at Pearl Harbor by the Empire of _____.

8. This world war changed Americans in ways no one had ever predicted. We were forever part of the world community. _____ was no longer an option.

9. During the early years of the war, most Americans were afraid that Japan or Germany might invade the United States, so the federal government felt that it needed to relocate thousands of _____-Americans.

10. More than _____ million people died in World War II.

Assignment (Each answer is worth 10 points.)

True / False:

1. Most Jewish children were spared the horrors of the Holocaust. T/F

2. Following the invasion of the Soviet Union in June 1941, Einsatzgruppen (mobile killing units) initiated mass-murder operations against Jewish people and Gypsies. T/F

3. Nazi German authorities deported millions of Jews from Germany, from occupied territories, and from the countries of many of its Axis allies. T/F

4. Deported Jews were brought to ghettos and to killing centers, often called extermination camps. T/F

5. Jews and others were murdered in specially developed gassing facilities. T/F

Fill in the Blank:

6. The Holocaust was the systematic, state-sponsored _____ of approximately six million Jews by the Nazi regime and its collaborators from 1933 to 1945.

7. The National Socialist Party, Nazis, who came to power in Germany in January 1933, believed that Jews were "_____."

8. German authorities also targeted other groups because of their perceived "racial inferiority": Roma (Gypsies), the _____, and some of the Slavic peoples (Poles, Russians, and others).

9. Other groups were persecuted on political, _____, and behavioral grounds, among them Communists, Pentecostals, Socialists, Jehovah's Witnesses, and homosexuals.

10. In 1933, the Jewish population of Europe stood at over eight million, with most European Jews living in countries that Nazi Germany would _____ or influence during World War II.

Assignment (Each answer is worth 10 points.)

True / False:

1. The Yalta conference is often cited as the beginning of the Cold War. T/F

2. President Roosevelt was hoping the future United Nations organization would be the place to deal with Hitler. T/F

3. Negotiations 1945: World War II ends and the allies were in agreement over the way Europe should develop. T/F

4. Demonstration 1946: The Cold War transformed Harry Truman. T/F

5. Containment 1947–1949: Truman committed American resources to any nation that was opposed to Communism. T/F

Fill in the Blank:

6. Coercion 1950–1968: America fights a war against North Korea, joins the race to the moon, and enters the _____ War.

7. _____ 1968–1980: With the end of the Vietnam War, President Nixon invites a cooling of relations with the Soviet Union, which was exhausted by the expensive arms race.

8. Confrontation 1980–1985: President Ronald Reagan forces the Soviet Union to enter a costly _____ race.

9. Glasnost 1985–1989: By this point, it was clear to the Soviet Union that accommodation and _____ were necessary or the country's economy would collapse.

10. Revolution 1989–1991: The _____ Wall falls and communism ends in the Soviet Union.

Assignment (Each answer is worth 10 points.)

True / False:

1. The Korean War has been called the "Lost War." T/F

2. The Korean War was one of the final hot wars of the Cold War. T/F

3. Truman, MacArthur, Mao, and Stalin were strangely absent from the war. T/F

4. The Korean War began in the early hours of June 1950. T/F

5. North Korean troops crossed the 38th parallel and invaded South Korea. T/F

Fill in the Blank:

6. The South Korean army was driven south to the end of the peninsula. Only when the U.S. Army intervened could the _____ forces be stopped.

7. The war involved some of the most _____ fighting ever experienced by American soldiers.

8. Within three years, _____ American servicemen lost their lives — most of them during the first critical year.

9. This was a significantly higher figure per year than the almost _____ American casualties spread over ten years in Vietnam.

10. Although an _____ was signed in 1953 between the U.S., China, and North Korea, South Korea refused to sign it, leaving the two Koreas in a state of war to the present.

Continue work on body paragraphs and revise your intro. As you do so, look carefully at your thesis. Is it succinct? Can you argue for the truth in it?

If you chose a creative project, take your course time to work on it.

Assignment (Each answer is worth 10 points.)

True / False:

1. The Vietnam War (although it was never formally a "war") was waged for control of South Vietnam by North Vietnam and its allies against South Vietnam, the United States, and their allies. T/F

2. At various times, the U.S. and ARVN forces were supported by Australian, South Korean, New Zealand, Thai, and Filipino troops. T/F

3. The principal opposition was the North Vietnamese People's Army of Viet Nam and the Viet Cong military wing of the National Front for the Liberation of South Vietnam. T/F

4. U.S. military advisers came to the south at the start of the war. T/F

5. These advisors began to accompany South Vietnamese combat troops in 1962. T/F

Fill in the Blank:

6. The Gulf of _____ incident in 1964 signaled the beginning of open combat involvement.

7. Major introductions of U.S. _____ combat troops came in 1965.

8. As Vietnamization began, and the _____ Peace Talks were completed in 1972, the U.S. role changed again. South Vietnam fought its own ground war, with U.S. ground combat troops withdrawing between 1968 and 1972.

9. The U.S. provided limited replacements of supplies and maintained a large diplomatic Defense Attaché Office that monitored the ARVN until the fall of South Vietnam in _____.

10. Other than for the immediate security of the evacuation, no U.S. combat troops or aircraft had been in South Vietnam since 60 days after the signing of the peace _____.

Assignment (Each answer is worth 10 points.)

True / False

1. Poland was deluged with books, magazines, newspapers, video documentaries, and radio broadcasts. T/F

2. Reagan lifted sanctions against Poland on February 19, 1987, and the Pope praised Solidarity on his trip to Poland in June. T/F

3. Against Gorbachev's urging, on April 5, 1989, the Polish Communist government legalized Solidarity. T/F

4. Within a year, communist rule ended in Eastern Europe and the Soviet Union. T/F

5. Walesa was a deeply ingrained existentialist. T/F

Fill in the Blank

6. The most important cause of the end of the Cold War was the _____ resistance to communism by the people of Eastern Europe.

7. Movements like _____ were the real reason that communist governments found themselves undermined and vulnerable.

8. It was the mass of working men and women in Europe that made possible the free _____, the collapse of the Berlin Wall, and the disappearance of the Iron Curtain that signified the end of the Cold War.

9. It was also the prayer and fasting of a great number of _____ believers, inside and outside the Iron Curtain.

10. Lech Walsea was the leader of the Solidarity resistance who organized the shipyard and dock workers into a powerful labor movement that was _____ December 13, 1981.

Assignment (Each answer is worth 10 points.)

True / False:

1. By 1945, Russia was the strongest nation in the world. T/F

2. The tyranny of Nazi fascism was quickly replaced by Soviet hegemony. T/F

3. After World War II, five nations arose as new global powers. T/F

4. There were now only two superpowers. T/F

5. The traditional school argued that Soviet aggression and imperialism were the fundamental cause of the Cold War. T/F

Fill in the Blank:

6. Americans looked to the future with hope and optimism; however, all these hopes were dashed with the advent of _____ imperialism.

7. For the first time in history, a country had the technological means to _____ world civilization.

8. The _____ school was reticent to place all the blame on the Soviet Union.

9. Many came to the conclusion that the United States _____ ambition was partly responsible for the Cold War.

10. The new _____ school found America exclusively responsible for the Cold War, since the Cold War offered Americans a chance to expand their economic hegemony over the world and Americans pursued their selfish aims with ingenuity and enthusiasm.

Assignment (Each answer is worth 10 points.)

True / False:

1. Absurdism is a worldview/philosophy that argues that each individual is his own world. T/F

2. Elie Wiesel was born in 1928 and lived through one of the most horrible periods in history. T/F

3. During World War II, he, with his family and other Jews from Romania, were sent to Auschwitz concentration camp where his parents and little sister were gassed and cremated. T/F

4. Wiesel only grew in his faith through his experiences. T/F

Fill in the Blank:

5. "There are two kinds of existentialists; first, those who are Christian . . . and on the other hand the _____ existentialists, among whom . . . I class myself."

6. "What they have in common is that they think that _____ precedes essence, or, if you prefer, that subjectivity must be the turning point."

7. It is not that someone tells the truth because he is _____, but rather he defines himself as honest by telling the truth again and again.

8. "Nowhere is it written that the _____ exists, that we must be honest, that we must not lie."

9. "Indeed, everything is _____ if God does not exist."

10. _____ is the central and unique potentiality that makes us uniquely human. Therefore, to abdicate that role, and to submit oneself to a higher authority — e.g., God — is to act in an inhuman way.

Spend the next two Fridays finishing up the first draft of your body paragraphs.

If you chose a creative project, take your course time to work on it.

Assignment (Each answer is worth 10 points.)

True / False:

1. The prison system has few African American men inside it. T/F

2. Two-thirds of African American children are born to unwed mothers. T/F

3. When talking about racism, white people often define it in systemic terms. T/F

4. When some African Americans talk about racism, they describe and define it in personal terms. T/F

5. Black nationalism was a movement among African Americans whose primary purpose was to define and to celebrate African American culture and heritage. T/F

Fill in the Blank:

6. The early civil rights movement sought to _____ blacks into American society; black nationalism oftentimes sought to bring blacks out of American culture.

7. Booker T. Washington offered a nonviolent celebration of "_____" and called for his country to embrace a form of separatism and black pride.

8. Black nationalists felt that the _____ Rights movement did not go far enough to improve black conditions.

9. Gains by the civil rights movement were mitigated by _____, by welfare, and by persistent racism.

10. Black nationalist strategies called for the _____ of African American–controlled economic and political institutions.

Assignment (Each answer is worth 10 points.)

True / False:

1. Separatism was the main tactic embraced by black nationalism. T/F

2. Some African Americans concluded that attempts at reconciliation were too late, that white America's apostasy was too great to be redeemed. T/F

3. By 1970, many African American thinkers, religious leaders, social workers, and politicians were patiently biding their time. T/F

4. Black Power consciously avoided the historical reality of America's prejudice. T/F

5. The black community moved from nonviolent resistance to violent resistance because African Americans saw themselves in an intolerable state. T/F

Fill in the Blank:

6. This violence was _____ by the April assassination of Martin Luther King Jr., but frustration had been brewing in the African American heart for years.

7. The Black Panthers wanted immediate results and were not willing to wait for legal and legislative processes. They wanted _____, not gradualism.

8. Malcolm X and Louis Farrakhan began the controversial Nation of Islam or African American _____.

9. Martin Luther King Jr., called for _____ and nonviolence, assimilation and peaceful coexistence.

10. By the 1990s, within the African American community the marriage of race and power was secure. Equality was no longer a goal: _____ was.

Assignment (Each answer is worth 10 points.)

True / False:

1. Racism created a cycle of wealth in northern urban ghettos. T/F

2. Other ethnic groups (e.g., Chicanos, Puerto Ricans, Asians) fared worse in the upward mobility trek than did African Americans. T/F

3. The number and proportion of African American skilled workers continued to increase over time. T/F

4. The African American community was not without its strengths, but the strengths were constantly compromised. T/F

5. May 17, 1954, Brown vs. The Board of Education, was a momentous day in the history of the world: a nation voluntarily acknowledged and repudiated its own oppression of part of its own people. T/F

Fill in the Blank:

6. The civil rights movement sought _____ by demanding that racism cease to be a significant category.

7. "Some may more quietly commemorate the suffering, struggle, and sacrifice that has triumphed over much of what is wrong with the original document [the U.S. Constitution], and observe the anniversary with hopes not _____ and promises not fulfilled." (Justice Thurgood Marshall)

8. African American culture had grown terribly _____ by the late 1990s.

9. Viktor E. Frankl, a survivor of the Nazi concentration camps, observes, "A man who could not see the end of his 'provisional existence' was not able to aim at an _____ existence."

10. _____ should not be a source of power and advantage or disadvantage in a Christian, free society.

Assignment (100 points possible)

Write a personal reflection of this account, noting your own feelings and beliefs over what a Christian community should be like to strangers of any background who come to find the grace of Christ.

Final week of working on first draft of body paragraphs. Emphasize broad strokes for this first run through.

If you chose a creative project, take your course time to work on it.

Take your third quarterly exam.

Assignment (Each answer is worth 10 points.)

True / False:

1. Martin Luther King Jr., (1929–1968), civil rights leader, American humanitarian, pastor, and Nobel Peace Prize winner, was one of the premier history makers of the 20th century. T/F

2. He was not only one of the principal leaders of the American civil rights movement, he was also a prominent advocate of violent protest. T/F

Fill in the Blank on these lines from the "I Have a Dream" speech:

3. Instead of honoring this sacred obligation, America has given the Negro people a bad check which has come back marked "insufficient funds." But we refuse to believe that the bank of _____ is bankrupt.

4. Now is the time to rise from the dark and desolate valley of segregation to the sunlit path of _____ justice.

5. We must not allow our creative protest to degenerate into physical violence. Again and again we must rise to the majestic heights of meeting physical force with _____ force.

6. I have a dream that my four children will one day live in a nation where they will not be judged by the color of their skin but by the content of their _____.

7. I have a dream that one day every valley shall be exalted, every hill and mountain shall be made low, the rough places will be made plain, and the crooked places will be made straight, and the glory of the Lord shall be revealed, and all flesh shall see it _____.

8. Five score years ago, a great American, in whose symbolic shadow we stand, signed the _____ Proclamation.

9. One hundred years later, the life of the Negro is still sadly crippled by the manacles of _____ and the chains of discrimination.

10. When the architects of our republic wrote the magnificent words of the Constitution and the Declaration of Independence, they were signing a promissory note to which every _____ was to fall heir.

Assignment (Each answer is worth 10 points.)

True / False:

1. John Perkins is an outspoken born-again Christian who unapologetically argues that faith in Christ is the hope of both the white and black communities. T/F

2. In 1960, John Perkins, his wife Vera Mae, and their children left a "successful" life in California and moved back to Mendenhall, Mississippi, to begin ministry. T/F

3. The urban poor are oppressed, observes Perkins, by external forces alone. T/F

4. Perkins helps readers rethink their assumptions about what inner-city ministry should be and relates what the Bible says it is. T/F

5. Malcom X had a typically happy childhood, coloring his later views of humanity. T/F

Fill in the Blank:

6. Malcolm X was born Malcolm _____ on May 19, 1925, in Omaha, Nebraska.

7. His father, Earl Little, was an outspoken Baptist minister and avid supporter of black nationalist leader Marcus _____.

8. Earl's civil rights activism prompted death threats from the white supremacist organization Black Legion, forcing the family to relocate twice before _____ fourth birthday.

9. Malcolm was taught the gospel and some people think that he made a commitment to _____.

10. By the early 1950s, Little was converted to _____ and took the name Malcolm X.

Assignment (Each answer is worth 10 points.)

True / False:

1. The black American family, as well as the black American church, has been trivialized for centuries. T/F

2. Welfare had a profoundly positive effect on African American communities. T/F

3. Social welfare, as it was conceived and implemented in American history, broke governmental norms by fixing the root of the issue. T/F

4. The black community entrusted its future to the American political, legal, and social welfare systems. T/F

5. The government never attacked the real cause of African American poverty. T/F

Fill in the Blank:

6. Some believe our social welfare policies are moving the African American community toward a sort of "_____," defined in Webster as a situation "in which conditions and the quality of life are dreadful."

7. When New York Senator Daniel Patrick Moynihan wrote his 1965 warning about the disintegration of the African American family, 26 percent of African American births were to unwed mothers. Today, that figure has soared to 68 percent and even higher (nearly _____ percent) in inner-city neighborhoods.

8. To the African American, the _____ represented a shattered dream.

9. The loss of fathers in African American families because of welfare dependency has had the most devastating effect on the _____ community.

10. Roosevelt's New Deal and Johnson's Great Society failed, on one hand, because they ignored the most fundamental need of all disadvantaged people: _____.

Assignment (100 points possible)

Write a personal reflection of this account, noting your own feelings and beliefs over what it must have felt like to be surrounded by people filled with so much hate. What should be the response of those who follow Christ and desire to reflect His love in such communities all across the country?

Today will be devoted to revising the body paragraphs. Look for grammatical errors, but especially focus on carrying the thesis throughout the entire paper. Does each body paragraph support the thesis?

If you chose a creative project, take your course time to work on it.

Assignment (Each answer is worth 10 points.)

True / False:

1. The decade of the 1960s was a time of objectivity and godly living. T/F

2. Conformity and uniformity were watchmen on the walls of early 1950 American culture. T/F

3. Television contributed to the homogenizing trend by providing young and old with a shared experience reflecting accepted social patterns. T/F

4. It was an era of traditionalism in art and writing. T/F

5. Allen Ginsberg gained notoriety for his poem "Howl," a scathing critique of modern, mechanized civilization. T/F

Fill in the Blank:

6. Elvis Presley popularized African American _____ music and took it a step further. He in effect helped create a new music genre: rock and roll.

7. "Modern art" invited the participant to new levels of subjectivity and narcissism. Meaning resided in the _____, not in the artists, and Americans could find meaning in their own experiences rather than in socially accepted norms and rituals.

8. Most Americans accepted that fact that there were problems in the 1960s that could not be solved without government _____.

9. The youngest man ever to win the presidency was 43-year-old John F. _____.

10. Using his skills of persuasion and calling on the legislators' respect for the slain president, in 1964 President Johnson succeeded in gaining passage of the _____ Rights Bill.

Assignment (Each answer is worth 10 points.)

True / False:

1. The conservative reaction to the radicalism of the 1960s and 1970s was nearly nonexistent. T/F

2. Opposition to the 1973 Supreme Court decision, *Roe v. Wade*, which upheld a woman's right to an abortion, brought together a wide array of organizations and individuals. T/F

3. Catholics, political conservatives, and religious fundamentalists, most of whom regarded abortion under virtually any circumstances as tantamount to murder, were prepared to organize in support of politicians who agreed with their position — and against those who disagreed with it. T/F

4. Ronald Reagan narrowly missed winning the Republican nomination for president in 1976 before succeeding in 1980 and going on to win the presidency from Jimmy Carter. T/F

5. President Reagan's general pessimism and lack of stage presence lasted through his tenure as president. T/F

Fill in the Blank:

6. Despite his propensity for misstatements, Reagan was known as the "Great _____," primarily for his mastery of television.

7. President Reagan enjoyed unusually high popularity at the end of his second term in office, but under the terms of the U.S. _____, he could not run again in 1988.

8. George H.W. Bush was elected the 41st president of the United States, campaigning on a promise to continue the prosperity Reagan had brought; he also argued that his expertise could better support a strong _____ for the United States.

9. The Democratic Party's candidate, Michael Dukakis, claimed that less fortunate Americans were hurting economically and that the _____ had to help those people while simultaneously bringing the federal debt and defense spending under control.

10. Bill Clinton was elected president in 1990, and while America experienced significant prosperity in his two-term tenure, we also experienced unprecedented political and _____ abuse of the office.

Assignment (100 points possible)

When the term "ecology" became popular, many resisted proposed measures to clean up the nation's air and water. Solutions would cost money for businesses and individuals, and force changes in the way people lived or worked. However, in 1970, Congress amended the Clean Air Act of 1967 to develop uniform national air-quality standards. It also passed the Water Quality Improvement Act, which made cleaning up offshore oil spills the responsibility of the polluter. Then, in 1970, the Environmental Protection Agency was created as an independent federal agency to spearhead the effort to bring abuses under control. Write a personal response stating why you think the government should do more or less to protect the environment, and why you feel this is an important issue or one that takes too many resources from more important issues.

Assignment (Each answer is worth 10 points.)

Fill in the Blank:

1. It is said that private character has virtually no impact on _____ character; that what matters above all is a healthy economy.

2. It is said . . . that that moral authority is defined solely by how well a president deals with public policy matters; that America needs to become more European (read: more "sophisticated") in its attitude toward sex; that lies about sex, even under oath, don't really matter; that we shouldn't be "_____."

3. These arguments define us down; they assume a lower common denominator of behavior and _____ than we Americans ought to accept.

4. "_____" is a word that is out of favor these days, but it remains a cornerstone of democratic self-government.

5. It is what enables us to hold ourselves, and our leaders, to high _____. It is how we distinguish between right and wrong, noble and base, honor and dishonor.

6. _____ society must give public affirmation to principles and standards, categorical norms, notions of right and wrong.

7. Even though public figures often fall short of these standards— and we know and expect some will — it is nevertheless crucial that we pay _____ to them.

8. Once in a great while, a single national event provides insight into where we are and who we are and what we esteem. The Clinton presidency has provided us with a window into our times, our moral order, our understanding of _____.

9. Moral good and moral harm are very real things, and moral good or moral harm can come to a society by what it esteems and by what it _____.

10. Many people have been persuaded to take a benign view of the Clinton presidency on the basis of arguments that have attained an almost talismanic stature. . . . We need to say no to those arguments as loudly as we can — and yes to the American _____ they endanger.

Finish editing the body paragraphs. As you do so, pay special attention to the content. Is it coherent? Persuasive? Unified in its intention?

If you chose a creative project, take your course time to work on it.

Assignment (Each answer is worth 10 points.)

True / False:

1. At the end of World War II, American industry abandoned wartime industries to meet peacetime needs, with Americans buying frugally due to the war. T/F

2. Traditional values had a revival among all Americans, with the phrase "under God" added to the Pledge of Allegiance, and churches being filled. T/F

3. Gender roles were quickly debased. T/F

4. Highways were built to take people quickly from one place to another, bypassing small towns and helping to create shopping malls. T/F

5. Toys for leisure became very popular, like the Hula Hoop,® named after the hula dance that missionaries had seen in Hawaii. T/F

Fill in the Blank:

6. Some historians emphasize the _____ side of history — who was in power and who was not, while other historians look at all the wars — who won them and who didn't.

7. _____ historians look at the lives of people living this history — what they ate and drank, what they did for entertainment, and so forth.

8. The Soviet Union said the Hula Hoop® toy was an example of the "emptiness of American _____."

9. _____ created an American mass-media culture. Whether one lived in Topeka, Kansas, or New York City, one saw the same programs, same commercials.

10. Television promoted the _____ family.

Assignment (Each answer is worth 10 points.)

True / False:

1. From about the late 1970s to the present, home education, or homeschooling emerged in American social life. T/F

2. Homeschooling is to teach your children at home, or be taught at home rather than in the public or private school systems. T/F

3. Homeschoolers are struggling to get into modern colleges. T/F

4. Evangelicals (and Christian homeschoolers) generally subscribe to two strongly held propositions: that a return to Christian values is necessary if the moral confusion of our time is to be overcome, and that the Enlightenment should be held as a standard for moral behavior. T/F

5. Christian homeschoolers argue that the excessives of Enlightenment rationalism have sabotaged the certitude of traditional ethics and Christian theism that so strongly influenced Western culture. T/F

Fill in the Blank:

6. Human _____ and aspirations are greater than the world can satisfy, so it is reasonable to look elsewhere for that satisfaction.

7. _____ is the highest and best reality (a decidedly anti-Enlightenment notion) and its genesis and maintenance come exclusively from relationship with God alone.

8. Homeschooling families, with their sacrificial _____ for one another and the extravagant gift of time to one another, offer a radical path into this new way of looking at reality.

9. Homeschoolers are building a new generation of culture _____ the old-fashioned way: parents stay home and love the kids and, in the process, lay their lives down for all our futures.

10. Homeschooling has invited Americans to a comfortable marriage of _____ and transcendentalism that fares our culture and our nation well in the years ahead.

Assignment (Each answer is worth 10 points.)

True / False:

1. Television has become the pinnacle of the social and intellectual universe. T/F

2. TV has become so familiar and so thoroughly integrated with American culture that we no longer hear its faint hissing in the background or see the flickering gray light. T/F

3. TV's epistemology is easily recognized by the masses. T/F

4. The world of television is still strange to us, being relatively new. T/F

5. For the loss of the sense of the strange is a sign of adjustment, and the extent to which we have adjusted is a measure of the extent to which we have changed. T/F

Fill in the Blank:

6. Our culture's adjustment to the epistemology of television is by now almost complete; we have so thoroughly accepted its definitions of _____, knowledge, and reality that irrelevance seems to us to be filled with import, and incoherence seems eminently sane.

7. Television's conversations promote incoherence and triviality . . . television speaks in only one persistent voice — the voice of _____.

8. To enter the great television _____, one American cultural institution after another is learning to speak its terms.

9. Television, in other words, is _____ our culture into one vast arena for show business.

10. Postman writes, "We are by now into a second generation of children for whom television has been their first and most accessible _____ and, for many, their most reliable companion and friend."

Assignment (100 points possible)

Write an essay about someone in your life who has made a deep impact on you as a person, just as Billy Graham did to so many around the world.

Write the first draft of your conclusion, your final paragraph. As you write, remember to summarize your ideas without stating new facts.

If you chose a creative project, take your course time to work on it.

Assignment (Each answer is worth 10 points.)

True / False:

1. Whitehead abandoned the notion, strong in Western philosophy since Plato, that what is most malleable is most real. T/F

2. Reality was not based on Platonic "forms" but on "fluid experience." T/F

3. Whitehead's agnosticism is most evident in his understanding of bliss. T/F

4. [God is] creative in the only sense in which creation is given any meaning by our experience. T/F

5. Men thus literally create each other when they mold each other's character by education and friendship. T/F

Fill in the Blank:

6. Perhaps no single Christian _____ has done more to speak persuasively to the non-Christian world than C.S. Lewis.

7. A man who was merely a man and said the sort of things _____ said would not be a great moral teacher. He would be either a lunatic — on a level with the man who says he is a poached egg — or else he would be the Devil of Hell.

8. You can shut Him up for a fool, you can spit at Him and kill Him as a demon, or you can fall at His feet and call Him Lord and God. But let us not come with any patronizing nonsense about his being a great _____ teacher.

9. Alfred North Whitehead was a metaphysician whose worldview requires God, and who respects the cultural role of _____ institutions.

10. Whitehead preferred to work within society's institutions. Nonetheless, Whitehead appealed to direct _____.

Assignment (Each answer is worth 10 points.)

True / False:

1. Charles Fuller was born in Los Angeles, California. He graduated from Pomona College in 1910 and then studied at the Bible Institute of Los Angeles, where he later became chairman of the board. T/F

2. He was famous as the radio host and speaker of the *Old-Fashioned Revival Hour*, a weekly Sunday broadcast. T/F

3. From 1941 through 1958, audiences attended services that were broadcast live on the radio from the Long Beach Municipal Auditorium. T/F

4. Fuller was opposed to higher education. T/F

5. Charles Fuller was one of the great evangelical leaders of the 20th century. T/F

Fill in the Blank:

6. We find there are some scholarly men to be had, few of whom have the spiritual qualities which we believe to be necessary for _____ in this school.

7. But I believe that God has for us, somewhere, scholarly men who are deeply spiritual and who have great _____.

8. It may be God's plan that later you should take over the presidency of this school. . . . We shall be _____ very definitely about this, that if it is God's will, He shall so impress you.

9. We are on the eve of the _____ Revival.

10. Billy Graham is soon to be on the East Coast for a revival. Fuller speaks highly of this young man. "Billy Graham's meetings will close Sunday night. He has had a wonderful series of meetings, and I am sure he will prove a _____ in Boston too."

Assignment (Each answer is worth 10 points.)

True / False:

1. *Pax Americana* is the term describing a relative military peace in the Western world. T/F

2. Since the end of the Cold War, many Americans have regarded the United States to be one of many superpowers. T/F

3. After 1990, America's political status has been a strong socialist presence in virtually every geopolitical theater in the world. T/F

4. Arguably, from 1945 to today, America has wielded influence by supporting left-wing dictatorships in undeveloped countries and democracies in developed countries. T/F

5. America is a nation builder. T/F

Fill in the Blank:

6. Today, America has the largest _____ in the world.

7. America had the largest nuclear _____ in the world during the first half of the Cold War.

8. American TV, American movies, and American fashion dominate world _____.

9. The decade from 2000 to 2010 was marked generally by an escalation of the social issues from the end of the 1990s — the rise of terrorism, the expansion of telecommunications with mobile phones, and the _____.

10. In spite of the terrorist attacks on September 11, 2001, America remains the most influential political, military, and _____ force in the world.

Assignment (Each answer is worth 10 points.)

Fill in the Blank:

1. Prediction is _____, particularly in a world where one scientific advance can change a whole era.

2. By the year 2000, despite a _____ birth rate, the present 200 million people will have grown to 300 million.

3. Many Americans will live well beyond _____ age . . . many beyond age 80.

4. The _____ will transform America.

5. Third world countries will emerge as new _____ powers.

6. As the world's richest nation, the United States will face the responsibilities of power in a world where other nations, disturbed by our _____, will grasp every opportunity to force us to face our human responsibilities.

7. If we are impatient, we can set off an _____ war.

8. The exodus from farms to cities is almost over. Americans will move back into _____ areas.

9. The _____ will become more of an issue than ever.

10. The energy crisis of 1974–75 will be _____ in the next few decades.

Finish editing the body paragraphs. As you do so, pay special attention to the content. Is it coherent? Persuasive? Unified in its intention?

If you chose a creative project, take your course time to work on it.

Assignment (Each answer is worth 10 points.)

Fill in the Blank:

1. On September 11, 2001, four commercial airplanes were _____.

2. Two of the planes were deliberately crashed into the twin towers of the World Trade Center in New York City, one was deliberately crashed into the _____ in Washington, D.C., and the fourth crashed into a field in rural Western Pennsylvania, presumably on its way to a fourth symbolic target.

3. Strong evidence suggested that Osama bin Laden, a Saudi Arabian citizen living in Afghanistan, was behind the attacks. In 2003, bin Laden became the head of a terrorist organization known as al-Qaeda (Arabic for "the _____").

4. From 1998 to 2000, President Clinton pursued a policy of economic sanctions against the Taliban and sent numerous messages to the de facto government of _____, demanding that it deliver bin Laden for trial in the United States.

5. When George W. _____ took office in January 2001, it is doubtful that he understood the depth of bin Laden's hatred of America. Just eight short months later came the devastating September 11 attacks.

6. In 1998, bin Laden told his followers, "The call to wage war against America was made because America has spearheaded the crusade against the _____ nation."

7. This is a religious war against "_____ and unbelievers," in bin Laden's words.

8. When it became clear that bin Laden was the probable instigator of the attacks, Bush delivered an ultimatum to the _____ to turn over bin Laden or face the might of the U.S. military.

9. When intervention is required, the Bush Doctrine emphasizes action by _____ of the willing and able.

10. Military _____ is not the first choice for dissuading countries from backing terrorism with weapons of mass destruction, including chemical, biological, and nuclear weapons.

Assignment (Each answer is worth 10 points.)

True / False:

1. At the heart of much terrorism is militant Hinduism. T/F

2. At the heart of militant Islam is the Koran, the sacred book of Muslims. T/F

3. The Koran is regarded by Muslims as the revelation of God. T/F

4. Supplemented by the so-called Hadith, or traditions, it is the foundation of Islam. T/F

5. It is considered a supplementary authority on belief, worship, ethics, and social conduct. T/F

Fill in the Blank:

6. The name Koran, or better Qur'an, from the Arabic stem Qara'a, "to read," "to recite," means the "_____," the "Recitation," i.e., the "Book," par excellence.

7. It is also called "Alkitab" (The Book), "Furquan" (liberation, deliverance, of the revelation), "Kitab-ul-lah" (Book of God), "Al-tanzil" (The _____).

8. It consists of 114 _____ or chapters, some being almost as long as the Book of Genesis, others consisting of but two or three sentences.

9. It is smaller than the _____ Testament, and in its present form has no chronological order or logical sequence.

10. It is like reading *Meditations* by Marcus Aurelius or *Sayings* by _____.

Assignment (Each answer is worth 10 points.)

True / False:

1. President Obama was inaugurated as president in 2009. T/F

2. From the beginning of Obama's administration, he focused on the danger of terrorism. T/F

3. The images burned into the American heart hours after the attacks of September 11, 2001, are fading away. Obama's administration was bent on repairing the U.S. image among Muslim nations. T/F

4. In fact, during the tenth-year anniversary, the word "terrorism" is heavily used in Obama's vernacular. T/F

5. America, at the end of the first decade of the New Millennium, appeared to be in trouble. T/F

Fill in the Blank:

6. President Obama pledged to "go after" _____ and "win this fight."

7. There even was a tangential reference to a "_____ struggle" as the U.S. relentlessly pursues those who threaten the country.

8. In 2011, Osama bin Ladin was apprehended and killed by U.S. Navy _____.

9. On the domestic front, President Obama continued to battle double-digit _____.

10. In the middle of the Obama Administration, the national debt soared over 14 _____ dollars.

Assignment (Each answer is worth 10 points.)

True / False:

1. Walt Disney built his vision in the 1950s and early 1960s when the Cold War was at its height and the likelihood of nuclear disaster seemed high. T/F

2. He wanted Disneyland to be not just a theme park but a portal to a better time and a different world. T/F

3. In 2001, we're talking about 6,000 civilians dying in televised destruction, and 60,000 or 600,000 more murders to come, if the terrorists succeed. T/F

4. Radical Muslims have step-by-step followed Qur'anic principles in killing civilians and Christians. T/F

5. Terrorists claimed that civilians at the World Trade Center are enemies because communists purportedly control the world. T/F

Fill in the Blank:

6. Given the severity of the threat, enormously tightened _____ security is clearly essential.

7. In our current crisis, aliens from bin Laden's recruitment countries should at the least be required to _____ the FBI of all their travels.

8. Bin Laden has declared war on the United States, and those who support him should have no more rights than _____ cells had in the United States during World War II.

9. The battle against _____ spies that followed was generally necessary, even though it was given a bad name by Joe McCarthy during the 1950s.

10. We can learn from the past if we do not consider ourselves _____ to it.

This week will be dedicated to overall revisions of the paper. At this point, look for grammatical errors, all while making sure the overall flow of the paper is focused.

If you chose a creative project, review your work and add any final touches.

Assignment (Each answer is worth 10 points.)

(Note: Some of these responses are from pro-choice views and some are from pro-life views.)

Fill in the Blank:

1. Nearly all abortions take place in the first _____ [of pregnancy], when a fetus cannot exist independent of the mother.

2. Adoption is not an _____ to abortion because it remains the woman's choice whether or not to give her child up for adoption.

3. Abortion is a _____ medical procedure.

4. The ability of a woman to have control of her body is critical to _____ rights.

5. _____ dollars are used to enable poor women to access the same medical services as rich women, and abortion is one of these services.

6. Since life begins at _____, abortion is akin to murder as it is the act of taking human life.

7. No civilized society permits one human to intentionally harm or take the life of another human without _____.

8. An abortion can result in medical _____ later in life.

9. Those who choose abortions are often minors or young women with insufficient life _____ to understand fully what they are doing.

10. Abortion frequently causes intense _____ pain and stress.

Assignment (Each answer is worth 10 points.)

True / False:

1. Reconciliation is simply a relational problem. T/F

2. In spite of past mistakes, however, many Christians feel that Christianity is the key to racial reconciliation. T/F

3. Most Americans agree on one thing: racial reconciliation is a laudable goal. T/F

4. By dying on the Cross, Jesus paid the price for reconciliation with God. T/F

5. The doctrine of sin is the least empirically arguable doctrine of Christianity. T/F

Fill in the Blank:

6. Forgiveness is not about right or wrong, it is about _____, doing what God commands us to do.

7. Forgiveness begins with a remembering and moral _____.

8. Second, although the move toward forgiveness demands the renunciation of _____, it does not mean that the African American community abandons justice.

9. The gospel's central message is to _____ alienated people to God and to each other, across racial, cultural, and social barriers.

10. _____ was a clear goal for the early Church. After all, the example of the Cross drew all persons into hopeful relationship.

Assignment (Each answer is worth 10 points.)

True / False:

1. Elijah came home to Zion, to the City of God, to appease the gods of the age. T/F

2. Ahab and Jezebel were very capable, successful monarchs. From their perspective, they were the sanctioned leaders. Elijah and the prophets were radical, unreasonable, uncompromising troublers of Israel. T/F

3. Ahab and Jezebel could understand why Elijah would not carry on a civil discussion. T/F

4. This generation is the Elijah generation. To Elijah, the behavior of Ahab and Jezebel was absolutely appalling. While claiming to worship the Hebrew God, they also filled the land with syncretism, with apostate worship of the Baals. T/F

5. Elijah was not accommodating nor was he running away; he was coming home to challenge the gods of this age. T/F

Fill in the Blank:

6. In 1 Kings 18–19, the famous Mt. _____ challenge chapters, choleric Elijah is coming home — and no one wants him to come home.

7. After a long time, in the third year, the word of the Lord comes to Elijah: "Go and present yourself to _____, and I will send rain on the land" (1 Kings 18:1).

8. Even though Elijah brings good news — it is finally going to _____ — no one welcomes him. Elijah's fish-or-cut-bait prophetic messages are irritating the life out of the status quo.

9. "Once Americans had _____ and no technology to fulfill those dreams. Now Americans have tons of technology, but they have no dreams left." —Professor Harvey Cox

10. We have a chance, perhaps in our lifetime, to experience an unprecedented _____.

Assignment (Each answer is worth 10 points.)

True / False:

1. Philadelphia rapper The Ambassador performed for a hip hop forum. The forum sought to gather students to discuss the spiritual, racial, and social aspects of hip-hop. T/F

2. With the release of his album, *The Thesis*, Branch made history, debuting at no. 5 on the Billboard Gospel Charts, a noteworthy feat for a genre that is still an underground movement. T/F

3. According to Branch, Christian hip-hop is an oxymoron. T/F

4. You have to understand that God does not embrace anything that has a corrupt origin. T/F

5. We must be a part of the world in order to reach the world. T/F

Fill in the Blank:

6. It's not just music. It's a way of life for the black community as well as white America. It has _____ our youth in a way that no other tool of the enemy could have.

7. "The hip-hop community is one of the neediest, yet one of the most neglected by the community of _____ (the church)," Branch said.

8. We have termed it Christian hip-hop or holy hip-hop. That's our way of changing it. So, we don't change hip-hop. That's just another _____ topic.

9. Wikipedia uses the following description for the musical style on its website: "Christian hip-hop has a history of being dismissed by churches world-wide as _____, or 'devil music.' "

10. We must be examples of true Christians in order to win the lost. We cannot _____ to be lost or conform to the world's standards because we want to appeal to them."

Having finished the paper or creative project, make sure that your sources are cited (any style works, as long as your teacher can effectively search the sources for the information you used) and then write a page of reflection on the process of writing your paper or creating your project.

Assignment (Each answer is worth 10 points.)

Fill in the Blank:

1. The right of a competent, terminally ill person to avoid excruciating pain and embrace a timely and dignified death bears the sanction of history and is implicit in the concept of ordered _____. (American Civil Liberties Union)

2. A state's categorical ban on physician assistance to suicide — as applied to competent, terminally ill patients who wish to avoid unendurable pain and hasten inevitable death — substantially _____ with this protected liberty interest and cannot be sustained. (American Civil Liberties Union)

3. The history of the law's treatment of assisted suicide in this country has been and continues to be one of the _____ of nearly all efforts to permit it. (Washington v. Glucksberg)

4. That being the case, our decisions lead us to conclude that the asserted "right" to _____ in committing suicide is not a fundamental liberty interest protected by the Due Process Clause. (Washington v. Glucksberg)

5. Activists often claim that laws against euthanasia and assisted suicide are government mandated _____. But this claim would be similar to saying that laws against selling contaminated food are government mandated starvation. (International Task Force on Euthanasia and Assisted Suicide)

6. Laws against euthanasia and assisted suicide are in place to prevent abuse and to _____ people from unscrupulous doctors and others. They are not, and never have been, intended to make anyone suffer. (International Task Force on Euthanasia and Assisted Suicide)

7. Especially with regard to taking life, _____ slope arguments have long been a feature of the ethical landscape, used to question the moral permissibility of all kinds of acts. . . . The situation is not unlike that of a doomsday cult that predicts time and again the end of the world, only for followers to discover the next day that things are pretty much as they were. (R.G. Frey)

8. In debates with those bioethicists and physicians who believe that euthanasia is both deeply _____ and also a logical way to cut healthcare costs, I am invariably scorned when I mention "the slippery slope." (Nat Hentoff)

9. When the states legalize the deliberate ending of certain lives — I try to tell them — it will eventually broaden the categories of those who can be put to death with impunity. I am told that this is nonsense in our age of highly advanced medical _____. (Nat Hentoff)

10. American advocates of euthanasia often point to the Netherlands as a model — a place where euthanasia is quasi-legal for patients who request it. . . . Yet the September 1991 official government Remmelink Report on euthanasia in the Netherlands revealed that at least 1,040 people die every year from _____ euthanasia. Their physicians were so consumed with compassion that they decided not to disturb the patients by asking their opinion on the matter. (Nat Hentoff)

Assignment (Each answer is worth 10 points.)

True / False:

1. In 1997, 2,500 scientists signed a statement saying climate change was a non-issue. T/F

2. Also in 1997, 2,700 economists — including eight Nobel Prize winners — agreed that "preventive steps are necessary" to prevent the economic problems that will result from severe climate change. T/F

3. In 1998, the leaders of the world's 1,000 largest corporations agreed that climate change is the most critical problem facing humanity. T/F

4. The endless stream of dire predictions of what was going to happen years or decades from now if we did not drastically reduce our CO_2 production by virtually shutting down the economies of the world appeared to be hard scientific fact. T/F

5. Popular journalists trump coupled sets of second-order partial differential equations every time. T/F

Fill in the Blank:

6. They also have a right to spin the news any direction they choose because that's what _____ of the press is all about.

7. We _____ aren't all shaped by the same cookie cutter, and that's a blessing.

8. "_____" cannot prove or disprove science . . . science must stand on its own.

9. On December 13, 2007, 100 scientists jointly signed an Open Letter to Ban Ki-Moon, Secretary-General of the United _____.

10. The letter requested that they cease the _____ global warming hysteria and settle down to helping mankind better prepare for natural disasters.

Assignment (Each answer is worth 10 points.)

True / False:

1. The healthcare debate has been exceptionally civilized, and middle-ground has been found across the board. T/F

2. Washington engages in war-room-like campaigns to prevail over their opponents. T/F

3. The answer is that the disagreement over what must be done to improve American healthcare is profound and largely irreconcilable. T/F

4. Moreover, the outcome of the battle will be highly consequential, not just for our system of financing and delivering healthcare, but also for our economy and democratic processes. T/F

5. Enrolling people in some form of healthcare is low on the totem pole for Democratic leaders. T/F

Fill in the Blank:

6. The real sticking point between the two sides is over how to allocate _____ in the healthcare sector.

7. The question healthcare reform advocates must answer is this: what _____ will be put in place to bring about continual improvement in the productivity and quality of patient care?

8. Proponents of a governmental process have an unbounded confidence in the ability of the federal _____ to centrally plan and control an extremely complex sector of the American economy.

9. Politicians are incapable of building what amounts to a government-administered "_____ provider network."

10. We can choose to rely entirely on the federal government to allocate resources in the healthcare sector, or we can choose to let consumers and suppliers make decisions in a decentralized marketplace with the government providing _____ and enforcing consumer protections.

Assignment (Each answer is worth 10 points.)

True / False:

1. The population problem is vast in our world today. T/F

2. Nick Eberstadt of Harvard's Center for Population Studies found that "the world's population growth peaked at 1.9 percent around 1970 and is now down to 1.7 percent." T/F

3. "In the not too distant future, there will be a disproportionate number of youths compared to the elderly." T/F (Glen Stocker)

4. "Because this will place a tremendous economic burden upon the nonelderly to care for our older citizens, there will be a growing advocacy for euthanasia." T/F (Glen Stocker)

5. Population grows fastest in the world's poorest countries. T/F

Fill in the Blank:

6. Falling _____ rates are generally associated with improved standards of living, increased life expectancy, and lowered infant mortality.

7. In the United States, 33 million people — one in _____ Americans — are below the official poverty line.

8. Poverty is a condition of chronic _____ and need at the family level.

9. The world's current and projected population growth calls for an increase in efforts to meet the needs for food, water, healthcare, technology, and _____.

10. In the poorest countries, massive efforts are needed to keep social and economic conditions from deteriorating further; any real advances in well-being and the quality of life are negated by further _____ growth.

Finish any last touches on the paper or creative project and submit it. Well done!

Take your fourth quarterly exam.

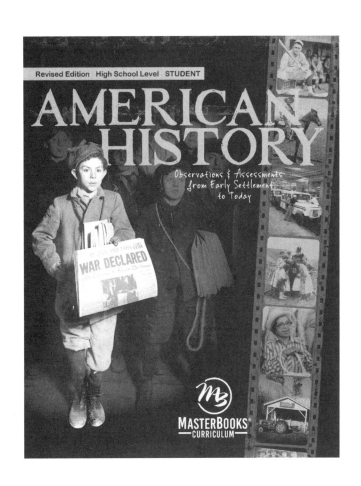

Quarterly Exams

for Use with

American History

Exam Questions (Each answer is worth 5 points.)

True / False:

1. Existentialism is an innately optimistic worldview. T/F

2. Virginia had the first African American slaves. T/F

3. Unlike the Pilgrims, the Puritans did not desire to separate themselves from the Church of England. T/F

4. The telling of history has remained basically the same since the start of the 20th century. T/F

5. Universities have changed little over the years in their attitudes toward Christians. T/F

6. Religious brotherhoods banded together and borrowed or furnished the funds necessary to pay the way to America. T/F

7. The Iroquois were perhaps the most politically powerful group of native people in the history of North America. T/F

8. The American Army—called the Continental army—never contained more than one-tenth of military-age Americans. T/F

9. The 13 colonies of America were tentatively held together by a document known as the Articles of Confederation. T/F

10. Thoreau was a frustrated pastor who gave up his faith, embraced Transcendentalism. T/F

Fill in the Blank:

biblical   Confederation   electoral   Intolerable   migration

philosophical   rationalism   slavery   valued   watershed

1. A worldview is a way that a person understands, relates to, and responds from a _____ position that he embraces as his own.

2. The tide of _____ that set in toward the shores of North America during the early years of the 17th century was but one phase in the restless and eternal movement of mankind upon the surface of the earth.

3. The institution of slavery had existed in Western Civilization since _____ times.

4. John Locke developed theories of human _____.

5. Women tended to be more highly _____ in America than in Europe.

6. The First Great Awakening was a _____ event in the life of the American people.

7. The _____ Acts were passed in 1774 to punish the colonists for the Boston Tea Party.

8. After a discussion lasting more than a year, the Articles of _____ were adopted by Congress, although the states did not ratify the Articles until 1781.

9. In 1836, Southern Congressmen passed a "gag rule" providing that the House automatically table petitions against _____, and Adams tirelessly fought the rule.

10. The president was elected by the _____ college chosen by state legislatures, not by direct voters.

Exam Questions (Each answer is worth 5 points.)

True / False:

1. Lockian rights excluded minorities, women, the poor, criminals, and organized laborers. T/F

2. In 1789, slavery was legal and practiced almost everywhere in the United States, which wouldn't change until the Civil War. T/F

3. The Awakening grew in the fragile air of pluralism. T/F

4. The Civil War was a struggle between conflicting worldviews. T/F

5. Economically, the Civil War was hard on the North, and led to it being an agrarian society for several more decades. T/F

6. The period called Reconstruction was between 1865 and 1877. T/F

7. Andrew Johnson was the first president to be impeached and was acquitted in the Senate by just one vote. T/F

8. Thomas Dixon's *The Clansman* presents racial conflict as an epic struggle, with the future of civilization at stake. T/F

9. Immigration played a key role not only in making America's development possible but also in shaping the basic nature of the society. T/F

10. The rise of American industry and immigration labor in the decades following the Civil War was short lived. T/F

Fill in the Blank:

abolitionist   Christians   conquered   opposed   pragmatism

protection   racial   restrict   scapegoat   teacher

1. Dorothea Dix was a _____ in Boston when she observed the mistreatment of a group of mentally challenged people in an 1841 jail.

2. Ultimately, Harriet Tubman joined the militant _____ cause and worked hard to end slavery.

3. "Dark and terrible as is this picture, I hold it to be strictly true of the overwhelming mass of professed _____ in America. They strain at a gnat, and swallow a camel." (Douglass)

4. Billy Graham was an outspoken supporter of _____ equality and social justice.

5. Lincoln changed later, but initially he, like the Republican Party, was _____ to slavery expansion, not to slavery.

6. Government claimed no right to do more than to _____ the territorial enlargement of it. (Lincoln)

7. Radical congressional Republicans wanted Southern states treated more like _____ provinces than wayward children.

8. John Dewey's views were known as "_____," which emphasizes action and results.

9. Immigrants became the _____ for the growing dislocation of urbanization and, during the Great Depression, the challenges of unemployment.

10. Laissez-faire policies stated that "the functions of the state should be limited to internal police and foreign _____ — no public education, no limitation of hours of labor, no welfare legislation."

Exam Questions (Each answer is worth 5 points.)

True / False:

1. The pietistic, revivalistic, and holiness Christian movements of the latter part of the 19th century were actively involving themselves in evangelical social work that was critical to the lives of thousands of average urban Americans. T/F

2. The West, its reality and myth, has played an important role in the formation of the American ethos. T/F

3. Jim Crow Laws were created after the Civil War by Northern states to control African Americans. T/F

4. There was little debate that an overseas empire was the right course of action for the U.S. T/F

5. Modern technologies, like radio and movies, promoted discipline and sacrifice, ultimately creating a more religious nation. T/F

6. Beauvoir, working from a philosophy called existentialism, argued that women should gain their identity from the Bible. T/F

7. To eliminate the possibility of the Soviet Union fighting if Poland were attacked, Hitler made a pact with the Soviet Union—the Nazi-Soviet Non-Aggression Pact. T/F

8. By 1945, Russia was the strongest nation in the world. T/F

9. Two-thirds of African American children are born to unwed mothers. T/F

10. The black community moved from nonviolent resistance to violent resistance because African Americans saw themselves in an intolerable state of shame. T/F

Fill in the Blank:

Dawes	gospel	intervene	Paris	reform
sinner	Solidarity	subculture	unemployment	Yellow

1. "Man is by nature a _____," Proudhon admitted, "that is to say not essentially a wrongdoer but rather wrongly made, and his destiny is perpetually to re-create his idea in himself."

2. The _____ Act of 1887 ended reservations and diminished the importance of the tribe/community by giving lands to individual tribal members.

3. Historians recognized that African American history was a _____ and needed to be examined separately from white American history.

4. _____ or exaggerated journalism, especially in New York newspapers owned by the competing publishers Joseph Pulitzer and William Randolph Hearst, was enormously successful in creating demand for U.S. intervention in Cuba.

5. The New Deal convinced most Americans that their government had a moral and legal right to _____ in public and private affairs if the general good of the public demanded it.

6. Some Christian leaders criticized Billy Sunday for putting too much emphasis on social policy (e.g., prohibition) and not putting enough emphasis on the _____ message.

7. Glasnost 1985–1989: By this point, it was clear to the Soviet Union that accommodation and _____ were necessary or the country's economy would collapse.

8. As Vietnamization began, and the _____ Peace Talks were completed in 1972, the U.S. role changed again. South Vietnam fought its own ground war, with U.S. ground combat troops withdrawing between 1968 and 1972.

9. Movements like _____ were the real reason that communist governments found themselves undermined and vulnerable.

10. Gains by the civil rights movement were mitigated by _____, by welfare, and by persistent racism.

Exam Questions (Each answer is worth 5 points.)

True / False:

1. Martin Luther King Jr. was not only one of the principal leaders of the American civil rights movement, he was also a prominent advocate of violent protest. T/F

2. The black community entrusted its future to the American political, legal, and social welfare systems. T/F

3. The conservative reaction to the radicalism of the 1960s and 1970s was nearly nonexistent. T/F

4. TV's epistemology is easily recognized by the masses. T/F

5. *Pax Americana* is the term describing a relative military peace in the Western world. T/F

6. At the heart of much terrorism is militant Hinduism. T/F

7. In spite of past mistakes, however, many Christians feel that Christianity is the key to racial reconciliation. T/F

8. The doctrine of sin is the least empirically arguable doctrine of Christianity. T/F

9. Nick Eberstadt of Harvard's Center for Population Studies found that "the world's population growth peaked at 1.9 percent around 1970 and is now down to 1.7 percent." T/F

10. Population grows fastest in the world's poorest countries. T/F

Fill in the Blank:

character   ghetto   creators   resources   psychological

Reading   social   suffering   superior   viewer

1. I have a dream that my four children will one day live in a nation where they will not be judged by the color of their skin but by the content of their _____.

2. To the African American, the _____ represented a shattered dream.

3. "Modern art" invited the participant to new levels of subjectivity and narcissism. Meaning resided in the _____, not in the artists, and Americans could find meaning in their own experiences rather than in socially accepted norms and rituals.

4. Homeschoolers are building a new generation of culture _____ the old-fashioned way: parents stay home and love the kids and, in the process, lay their lives down for all our futures.

5. In spite of the terrorist attacks on September 11, 2001, America remains the most influential political, military, and _____ force in the world.

6. The name Koran, or better Qur'an, from the Arabic stem Qara'a, "to read," "to recite," means the "_____," the "Recitation," i.e. the "Book," par excellence.

7. We can learn from the past if we do not consider ourselves _____ to it.

8. Abortion frequently causes intense _____ pain and stress.

9. Activists often claim that laws against euthanasia and assisted suicide are government mandated _____.

10. The real sticking point between the two sides is over how to allocate _____ in the healthcare sector.

Revised Edition High School Level STUDENT

AMERICAN HISTORY

Observations & Assessments from Early Settlement to Today

MASTERBOOKS® CURRICULUM

Answer keys

for Use with

American History

Chapter 1

Lesson 1

1. F
2. T
3. F
4. T
5. T
6. (a) Evangelicalism
7. (c) Worldview
8. (b) Christian homeschooling
9. philosophical
10. reality

Lesson 2

1. T
2. F
3. F
4. T
5. F
6. Delaware
7. Powhatans
8. Confederation
9. Clovis
10. hope

Lesson 3

1. F
2. F
3. T
4. T
5. F
6. government
7. captives
8. farmer
9. writing
10. Olmec

Lesson 4

1. F
2. T
3. T
4. F

5. F
6. flowers
7. slavery
8. Europeans
9. home
10. Pacific

Chapter 2

Lesson 1

1. T
2. F
3. F
4. T
5. F
6. Québec
7. Napoleon
8. praise
9. Mercantilism
10. 1608

Lesson 2

1. F
2. T
3. F
4. F
5. T
6. migration
7. Virginia
8. property
9. master
10. marry

Lesson 3

1. T
2. T
3. F
4. T
5. T
6. biblical
7. Racism
8. control

9. Africa
10. passively

Lesson 4
1. T
2. F
3. T
4. T
5. F
6. River
7. Amsterdam
8. Catholic
9. colonists
10. Maryland

Chapter 3

Lesson 1
1. T
2. F
3. T
4. F
5. F
6. Separatists
7. corn
8. good
9. Wampanoag
10. Thanksgiving

Lesson 2
1. T
2. F
3. F
4. T
5. F
6. Boston
7. Massachusetts
8. three
9. Baptist
10. separation

Lesson 3
1. F

2. T
3. T
4. F
5. F
6. Virginia – London Company
7. Plimouth Plantation – Pilgrims
8. New Hampshire and Maine – John Mason and Ferdinando Gorges
9. Massachusetts – Puritans
10. Connecticut – Massachusetts Colonists

Lesson 4
1. T
2. F
3. T
4. T
5. F
6. Puritans
7. Renaissance
8. philosophy
9. rationalism
10. blank

Chapter 4

Lesson 1
1. F
2. T
3. F
4. T
5. convention
6. valued
7. wife
8. legal
9. wife
10. planting/sowing

Lesson 2
1. T
2. T
3. F
4. England
5. emotional

6. covenant
7. Awakening
8. Sinners
9. Whitefield
10. watershed

Lesson 3
1. F
2. T
3. T
4. religious
5. evangelical
6. pastors
7. naturalistic
8. rationalism
9. intellectuals
10. intolerant

Lesson 4
1. T
2. F
3. F
4. T
5. revolution
6. chains
7. compromise
8. uneducated
9. Rousseau's
10. rights

Chapter 5

Lesson 1
1. T
2. F
3. T
4. F
5. intolerant
6. legislature
7. navy
8. Freeholders
9. dissenters

10. independence

Lesson 2
1. F
2. T
3. T
4. Intolerable
5. Quartering
6. Rousseau's
7. Navigation
8. Proclamation
9. Hobbes
10. Mercantilism

Lesson 3
1. F
2. T
3. F
4. F
5. arms
6. seven
7. warfare
8. British
9. Braddock
10. Duquesne

Lesson 4
1. F
2. T
3. T
4. F
5. surveying
6. Native American
7. murder
8. colonel
9. Mississippi
10. soldiers

Chapter 6

Lesson 1
1. T
2. F

3. T
4. F
5. Intolerable
6. rebellion
7. military
8. defend
9. Common
10. states

Lesson 2
1. T
2. F
3. T
4. northern
5. Washington
6. Declaration
7. Hessian
8. Congress
9. Confederation
10. Cornwallis

Lesson 3
1. T
2. F
3. F
4. T
5. T
6. broad
7. slavery
8. tyrants
9. influence
10. women

Lesson 4
1. T
2. F
3. T
4. F
5. Republic
6. revivals
7. conservative
8. slavery

9. communication
10. *Crucible*

Chapter 7
Lesson 1
1. T
2. F
3. F
4. T
5. agriculture
6. Shays
7. monarchy
8. Youth
9. Hamilton
10. Confederation

Lesson 2
1. F
2. T
3. T
4. F
5. T
6. executive
7. Senate
8. Rights
9. Alien
10. Amendments

Lesson 3
1. T
2. F
3. F
4. T
5. reason
6. action
7. soul
8. society
9. societies
10. duty

Lesson 4

1. F
2. T
3. Constitution
4. purpose
5. Nationalist
6. Progressives
7. Neoconservatives
8. Intellectuals
9. Left
10. five

Chapter 8

Lesson 1

1. T
2. F
3. F
4. T
5. criminals
6. Purchase
7. exploration
8. duel
9. 1803
10. Madison's

Lesson 2

1. nationalism
2. social
3. National
4. industrialization
5. transportation
6. Monroe
7. Jacksonian
8. Compromise
9. Erie
10. Feeling

Lesson 3

1. Adams
2. Representatives
3. civil
4. slavery

5. stroke

Short Answer

Answers will vary.

Lesson 4

1. T
2. F
3. T
4. T
5. F

Short Answer

Answers will vary.

Chapter 9

Lesson 1

1. F
2. T
3. T
4. F
5. Thoreau
6. Transcendentalism
7. preachers
8. Thoreau
9. Thoreau
10. Emerson

Lesson 2

1. electoral
2. parties
3. anxiety

Date	Hamiltonians	Jeffersonians
1791	Federalists	Democratic-Republicans
1824	National Republicans	Democratic-Republicans
1829	Republicans "Era of Good Feelings"	
1834	Whigs	Jackson Democrats
1840	Northern Whigs Anti-slavery Democrats	Southern Democrats
1854	Republicans	Democrats
Present	Republicans	Democrats

Lesson 3

1. F
2. T
3. T
4. T
5. nullification
6. splitting
7. monopoly
8. farmers
9. Nullification
10. national

Lesson 4

1. F
2. T
3. F
4. F
5. F
6. Union
7. annexation
8. democracy
9. spoils
10. slave

Chapter 10

Lesson 1

1. T
2. F
3. T
4. T
5. temperance
6. American
7. penitentiaries
8. solitary
9. right
10. Refuge

Lesson 2

1. T
2. F

3. T
4. Stanton
5. utopian
6. cooperative
7. Brook
8. worker
9. Dix
10. Wright

Lesson 3

1. teacher
2. ministry
3. outcast
4. God
5. endowments
6. 100,000
7. lobby
8. Congress
9. federal
10. philanthropic

Lesson 4

1. F
2. T
3. F
4. T
5. T
6. eternal
7. untruth
8. fear
9. equality
10. crowd

Chapter 11

Lesson 1

1. F
2. T
3. T
4. T
5. slave

6. evangelical

7. white-controlled

8. harbors

9. gin

10. Cotton

Lesson 2

1. T

2. F

3. abolitionist

4. 300

5. Moses

Short Answer: answers will vary

Lesson 3

1. T

2. F

3. T

4. slavery

5. abolished

Short Answer: answers will vary

Lesson 4

1. F

2. F

3. T

4. America

5. Christians

6. faith

7. heathen

Short Answer: answers will vary

Chapter 12

Lesson 1

1. F

2. T

3. T

4. T

5. F

6. *Democracy*

7. frontier

8. community

9. Awakening

10. Revivalism

Lesson 2

1. F

2. T

3. T

4. F

5. conversion

6. social

7. revivalism

8. Catholicism

9. racial

10. revivals

Lesson 3

Answers will vary but should include elements of the following from her account: It was in the middle of summer, but the service we were recommended to attend did not begin till it was dark. The sermon had considerable eloquence, but of a frightful kind. No image that fire, flame, molten lead, or red-hot pincers could supply; with flesh, nerves, and sinews quivering under them, was omitted. The other two priests arose, and began to sing a hymn. It was some seconds before the congregation could join as usual; every up-turned face looked pale and horror struck. And now in every part of the church a movement was perceptible, slight at first, but by degrees becoming more decided. They seated themselves on the "anxious benches." These whispers were inaudible to us, but the sobs and groans increased to a frightful excess. Young creatures, with features pale and distorted, fell on their knees on the pavement, and soon sunk forward on their faces; the most violent cries and shrieks followed. Violent hysterics and convulsions seized many of them, and when the tumult was at the highest, the priest who remained above, again gave out a hymn as if to drown it.

Lesson 4

1. T

2. T

3. T

4. F
5. F
6. sinners
7. law
8. grace
9. redemption
10. covenant

Chapter 13

Lesson 1
1. F
2. T
3. T
4. divorced
5. slavery
6. profitable
7. Whitney
8. water
9. European
10. farming

Lesson 2
1. T
2. T
3. F
4. F
5. F
6. foreigners
7. Brazil
8. expansion
9. opposed
10. personal

Lesson 3
1. T
2. F
3. F
4. T
5. T
6. Republican

7. Northerners
8. consensus
9. slave
10. Destiny

Lesson 4
1. F
2. T
3. T
4. T
5. F
6. utopia
7. laws
8. reason
9. passive
10. contribute

Chapter 14

Lesson 1
Research Day

Lesson 2
1. T
2. F
3. T
4. F
5. alone
6. army
7. draft
8. foreign
9. Emancipation
10. invaded

Lesson 3
1. T
2. F
3. T
4. F
5. T
6. fourteenth
7. bondmen

8. Cotton

9. tariff

10. Homestead

Lesson 4

1. F

2. T

3. final

4. remember

5. died

6. slaves

7. peculiar

8. restrict

9. Bible

10. charity

Chapter 15

Lesson 1

1. F

2. T

3. F

4. T

5. T

6. good

7. future

8. inconsistency

9. generation

10. opportunity

Lesson 2

1. T

2. T

3. F

4. T

5. F

6. Tennessee

7. Lincoln

8. conquered

9. Republican

10. Tennessee

Lesson 3

Answer will vary.

Lesson 4

1. F

2. T

3. T

4. T

5. F

6. prejudice

7. Babel

8. interracial

9. Jew

10. divisions

Chapter 16

Lesson 1

1. T

2. F

3. T

4. F

5. T

6. pardon

7. 4,000,000

8. amnesty

9. Texas

10. whites

Lesson 2

1. T

2. F

3. T

4. F

5. T

6. homogeneous

7. rehabilitation

8. bondage

9. guarded

10. vulture

Lesson 3

1. existence
2. dead
3. patriotism
4. Submission
5. slaves
6. power
7. Schurz
8. Stevens
9. Stevens
10. Schurz

Lesson 4

1. F
2. T
3. F
4. T
5. T
6. pragmatism
7. beliefs
8. environment
9. experience
10. ourselves

Chapter 17

Lesson 1

1. T
2. T
3. F
4. F
5. F
6. scapegoat
7. assimilation
8. expectations
9. Emigration
10. Immigration

Lesson 2

1. F
2. T

3. T
4. F
5. T
6. Protestant
7. Exclusion
8. native-born
9. Origins
10. 1900

Lesson 3

1. T
2. F
3. T
4. F
5. T
6. regularity
7. personal
8. dark
9. atheist
10. anthropological

Lesson 4

1. F
2. T
3. T
4. F
5. T
6. struggles
7. social
8. bourgeois
9. oppression
10. Proletariat

Chapter 18

Lesson 1

1. T
2. F
3. F
4. T
5. Railroad

6. labor
7. Spain
8. Homestead
9. Sherman
10. Commerce

Lesson 2
1. T
2. T
3. F
4. T
5. protection
6. Knights
7. Alien
8. Ten-Hour
9. 1883
10. Antitrust

Lesson 3
1. F
2. T
3. F
4. T
5. T
6. corporations
7. immigrants
8. Chamberlain
9. economic
10. morality

Lesson 4
1. F
2. T
3. F
4. T
5. T
6. elite
7. inevitable
8. revolution
9. continuity
10. profession

Chapter 19

Lesson 1
1. F
2. T
3. T
4. T
5. F
6. biblical
7. wealth
8. money
9. welfare
10. egalitarianism

Lesson 2
1. F
2. F
3. T
4. T
5. T
6. sinner
7. instinct
8. impulses
9. Anarchist
10. Chicago

Lesson 3
1. T
2. F
3. T
4. F
5. T
6. flood
7. Canal
8. steel
9. narrowed
10. earthen

Lesson 4
1. F
2. T
3. F

4. T

5. nation

6. business

7. independence

8. standard

9. fight

10. gold

Chapter 20

Lesson 1

1. T

2. F

3. F

4. T

5. T

6. frontier

7. land

8. gold

9. railroad

10. Irish

Lesson 2

1. F

2. T

3. F

4. F

5. T

6. Custer

7. Dawes

8. Howard

9. Geronimo

10. wronged

Lesson 3

1. T

2. F

3. F

4. F

5. T

6. conflict

7. James

8. minister

9. Confederate

10. legend

Lesson 4

1. F

2. T

3. T

4. T

5. revelation

6. altar

7. holier

8. invent

9. butcher

10. educate

Chapter 21

Lesson 1

1. F

2. T

3. T

4. T

5. F

6. currency

7. Ghettoization

8. racism

9. capitalistic

10. unskilled

Lesson 2

1. T

2. F

3. bucket

4. productions

5. race

6. strikes

7. prepared

8. opera

9. Exposition

10. justice

Lesson 3
1. F
2. T
3. T
4. F
5. Florida
6. Alabama
7. Virginia
8. Florida
9. Alabama
10. Alabama

Lesson 4
1. Maturation
2. Transition
3. Paternalism
4. transition
5. prejudice
6. subculture
7. Paternalism
8. Transition
9. Maturation
10. Accommodation

Chapter 22

Lesson 1
1. T
2. T
3. F
4. F
5. T
6. American
7. fittest
8. canal
9. isolationism
10. Yellow

Lesson 2
1. prosperous

2. decency
3. Monroe
4. Cuba
5. sympathy
6. violated
7. responsibility
8. humanity
9. sympathies
10. proper

Lesson 3
1. nationalist
2. Washingtons
3. fifty
4. afraid
5. Filipinos
6. years
7. homesick
8. looted
9. natives
10. weak

Lesson 4
1. Darwin
2. selection
3. Europe
4. Anglo-Saxon
5. Protestant
6. Roman-Catholic
7. Rome
8. supremacy
9. unheeded
10. God

Chapter 23

Lesson 1
1. T
2. T
3. F
4. F

5. T

6. Austro-Hungarian

7. neutrality

8. *Lusitania*

9. Germany

10. Allied

Lesson 2

1. T

2. F

3. T

4. T

5. F

6. Philippines

7. altruism

8. imperialism

9. isolationism

10. Darwinism

Lesson 3

1. F

2. T

3. T

4. T

5. F

6. cultural

7. Quality

8. threatened

9. compromise

10. leisure

Lesson 4

1. F

2. T

3. T

4. F

5. F

6. Stock

7. unemployment

8. tariff

9. Midwest

10. intervene

Chapter 24

Lesson 1

1. T

2. F

3. F

4. T

5. T

6. movies

7. Word

8. saloon

9. gospel

10. Graham

Lesson 2

1. T

2. F

3. F

4. T

5. T

6. needs

7. values

8. ideals

9. megalomaniac

10. poverty

Lesson 3

1. T

2. F

3. T

4. T

5. F

6. subservient

7. mind

8. Nazi

9. Enlightenment

10. existence

Lesson 4

1. T

2. F
3. T
4. T
5. F
6. stylish
7. club
8. bachelor
9. offspring
10. parties

Chapter 25

Lesson 1
1. T
2. F
3. F
4. T
5. T
6. 1870s
7. Japan
8. Isolationism
9. Japanese
10. 46

Lesson 2
1. F
2. T
3. T
4. T
5. T
6. murder
7. inferior
8. disabled
9. ideological
10. occupy

Lesson 3
1. T
2. F
3. F
4. T

5. T
6. Vietnam
7. Détente
8. arms
9. reform
10. Berlin

Lesson 4
1. F
2. F
3. F
4. T
5. T
6. Communist
7. difficult
8. 34,000
9. 60,000
10. armistice

Chapter 26

Lesson 1
1. T
2. T
3. T
4. F
5. T
6. Tonkin
7. ground
8. Paris
9. 1975
10. treaty

Lesson 2
1. T
2. T
3. F
4. T
5. F
6. grassroots
7. Solidarity

8. elections
9. Christian
10. suppressed

Lesson 3
1. F
2. T
3. F
4. T
5. T
6. Soviet
7. destroy
8. revisionist
9. expansionist
10. left

Lesson 4
1. F
2. T
3. T
4. F
5. atheistic
6. existence
7. honest
8. Good
9. permissible
10. Freedom

Chapter 27

Lesson 1
1. F
2. T
3. F
4. F
5. T
6. assimilate
7. blackness
8. Civil
9. unemployment
10. development

Lesson 2
1. T
2. T
3. F
4. F
5. T
6. precipitated
7. revolution
8. Muslims
9. reconciliation
10. empowerment

Lesson 3
1. F
2. F
3. F
4. T
5. T
6. equality
7. realized
8. disillusioned
9. ultimate
10. Race

Lesson 4
Answers will vary.

Chapter 28

Lesson 1
1. T
2. F
3. justice
4. racial
5. soul
6. character
7. together
8. Emancipation
9. segregation
10. American

Lesson 2
1. T
2. T
3. F
4. T
5. F
6. Little
7. Garvey
8. Malcolm's
9. Christ
10. Islam

Lesson 3
1. F
2. F
3. F
4. T
5. T
6. dystopia
7. 80
8. ghetto
9. black
10. employment

Lesson 4
Answers will vary.

Chapter 29
Lesson 1
1. F
2. T
3. T
4. F
5. T
6. soul
7. viewer
8. help
9. Kennedy
10. Civil

Lesson 2
1. F
2. T
3. T
4. T
5. F
6. Communicator
7. Constitution
8. defense
9. government
10. moral

Lesson 3
Answers will vary.

Lesson 4
1. governing
2. judgmental
3. leadership
4. Judgment
5. standards
6. Civilized
7. tribute
8. citizenship
9. disdains
10. ideals

Chapter 30
Lesson 1
1. F
2. T
3. F
4. T
5. T
6. political
7. Social
8. culture
9. Television
10. ideal

Lesson 2
1. T
2. T
3. F
4. F
5. T
6. needs
7. Worth
8. love
9. creators
10. intellectualism

Lesson 3
1. F
2. T
3. F
4. F
5. T
6. truth
7. entertainment
8. conversation
9. transforming
10. teacher

Lesson 4
Answers will vary.

Chapter 31

Lesson 1
1. F
2. T
3. F
4. T
5. T
6. writer
7. Jesus
8. human
9. religious
10. experience

Lesson 2
1. T
2. T
3. T
4. F
5. T
6. teachers
7. vision
8. praying
9. Great
10. blessing

Lesson 3
1. T
2. F
3. F
4. F
5. T
6. economy
7. arsenal
8. culture
9. Internet
10. social

Lesson 4
1. risky
2. declining
3. retirement
4. computer
5. world
6. dominance
7. atomic
8. rural
9. environment
10. repeated

Chapter 32

Lesson 1
1. highjacked
2. Pentagon

3. base

4. Afghanistan

5. Bush

6. Islamic

7. unbelief

8. Taliban

9. coalitions

10. intervention

Lesson 2

1. F

2. T

3. T

4. T

5. F

6. Reading

7. Revelation

8. suras

9. New

10. Confucius

Lesson 3

1. T

2. F

3. T

4. F

5. T

6. extremists

7. twilight

8. SEALS

9. unemployment

10. trillion

Lesson 4

1. T

2. T

3. T

4. F

5. F

6. homeland

7. notify

8. Nazi

9. Communist

10. superior

Chapter 33

Lesson 1

1. trimester

2. alternative

3. safe

4. civil

5. Taxpayer

6. conception

7. punishment

8. complications

9. experience

10. psychological

Lesson 2

1. F

2. T

3. T

4. T

5. F

6. atonement

7. judgment

8. vengeance

9. reconcile

10. Integration

Lesson 3

1. F

2. T

3. F

4. T

5. T

6. Carmel

7. Ahab

8. rain

9. dreams

10. revival

Lesson 4

1. T
2. T
3. F
4. T
5. F
6. influenced
7. faith
8. earthly
9. sacrilegious
10. appear

Chapter 34

Lesson 1

1. liberty
2. interferes
3. rejection
4. assistance
5. suffering
6. protect
7. slippery
8. compassionate
9. ethics
10. involuntary

Lesson 2

1. F
2. T
3. T
4. F
5. T
6. freedom
7. humans
8. Debate
9. Nations
10. man-made

Lesson 3

1. F
2. T

3. T
4. T
5. F
6. resources
7. process
8. government
9. preferred
10. oversight

Lesson 4

1. F
2. T
3. F
4. T
5. T
6. fcrtility
7. eight
8. deprivation
9. education
10. population

Quarterly Exam Answer Key

Quarterly Exam 1

1. F
2. T
3. T
4. F
5. F
6. T
7. T
8. T
9. T
10. F

1. philosophical
2. migration
3. biblical
4. rationalism
5. valued
6. watershed
7. Intolerable
8. Confederation
9. slavery
10. electoral

Quarterly Exam 2

1. F
2. F
3. T
4. T
5. F
6. T
7. T
8. T
9. T
10. F

1. teacher
2. abolitionist

3. Christians
4. racial
5. opposed
6. restrict
7. conquered
8. pragmatism
9. scapegoat
10. protection

Quarterly Exam 3

1. T
2. T
3. F
4. F
5. F
6. F
7. T
8. F
9. T
10. T

1. sinner
2. Dawes
3. subculture
4. Yellow
5. intervene
6. gospel
7. reform
8. Paris
9. Solidarity
10. unemployment

Quarterly Exam 4

1. F
2. T
3. F
4. F

5. T
6. F
7. T
8. F
9. T
10. T

1. character
2. ghetto
3. viewer
4. creators
5. social
6. Reading
7. superior
8. psychological
9. suffering
10. resources

Appendix

	Grading Rubric
Thesis ____ x 5 = ____	1. The thesis is ill-defined or missing 2. The thesis is there but is not followed throughout the paper, or is poorly thought out 3. The thesis is solid and followed throughout the paper, though not entirely inspired 4. The thesis is strong, consistently portrayed throughout the paper, and goes above standard expectations
Content ____ x 5 = ____	1. The content is lacking, as there is very little focus on the thesis, instead going off on tangents unrelated to the topic at hand 2. The content is there, but there isn't enough depth, and it lacks creativity 3. Content is strong but doesn't go far enough to establish a compelling argument 4. Content effectively conveys the message of the thesis and goes further than needed in order to present an interesting case
Grammar and punctuation ____ x 5 = ____	1. Poor handling of grammar conventions and punctuation 2. Average control of grammar and punctuation, though mistakes are still common 3. Adequate control of sentence structure and punctuation, with a few mistakes 4. Very few mistakes and artful use of punctuation; excellent grammar usage
Organization ____ x 5 = ____	1. Poor use of transitions, lack of overall organization; little thought went into the structure 2. Transitions need work, the paper is somewhat poorly organized 3. Adequate job on transitions and organization of content, with ideas being connected to each other 4. Masterful use of transitions, ideas flow into each other exceedingly well, and the organization of the paper excellent
Style ____ x 5 = ____	1. Poor sentence structure, repeated word choices, or uninspired words used, and poor citation of sources 2. Okay sentence structure, but something is lacking; word choice is still uninspired, but acceptable; citation is adequate 3. Good sentence structure and word choice, as well as good citation of sources 4. Excellent sentence structure, word choice, and citation of sources

Total
Score _____
100 possible points

Eight Major Worldviews

	Summary	Spiritual Influence	Examples	References
Theism	Believe God is personally involved with humankind.	Since the dawn of history, the world had been motivated by a theistic vision. Theism argued for a worldview in which God was in control of everything, and His moral precepts were critical to human conduct. This was the only viable worldview until the Renaissance.	Homer, Virgil, C.S. Lewis, A.J. Cronin, J.R.R. Tolkien	Chapters 1, 3 and 30
Deism	Believe God was present but is no longer present.	The world is said to be like a clock wound up by God many years ago, but He is now absent. The clock (i.e., the world) is present; God is absent. Still, though, deism embraced a Judeo-Christian morality.	Albert Einstein, Voltaire	Chapters 1, 2, and 3
Romanticism	Believe God is or was nature.	Romanticism stated that God was nature, and "it" was good. The more natural things were, the better. Nature was inherently good. Nature alone was the ultimate reality. In other words, nature was the romantic god.	James Fenimore Cooper, Goethe	Chapters 1, and 9
Naturalism	Believe that if God exists, He is pretty wimpy.	Only the laws of nature have any force. God is either uninterested or downright mean. All reality was reducible to impersonal processes and energy events.	Epicurus, Ernest Nagel	Chapters 1 and 16
Realism	Believe in a world with no purpose.	Realism sees a world with no purpose, no meaning, no order. Realism uses terms like "dignity" and "human rights" and "power." What realists mean, however, is that these concepts are real when they fulfill a social agenda that enhances human dominance over the universal.	Plato, Amit Goswami	Chapter 1
Absurdism	Believe there is no god nor any reason to have one.	A modern movement where everything is disorganized and anarchy rules. There is a complete abandonment of explaining the cosmos and, therefore, an abandonment of being in relationship with the deity.	Albert Camus, Kurt Vonnegut, Jr.	Chapter 1
Existentialism	Believe everything is relative.	The submergence of God in overwhelming data and in experience is the first step toward believing that God is dead. In this very pessimistic worldview, truth is open to debate.	Franz Kafka, Jean-Paul Sartre, Nietzsche	Chapter 1, 10, 24, and 26
Postmodernism	Believe in the rejection of objective truth.	In postmodernism, every sacred belief and ethic is in question. Before postmodernism, the Golden Rule, for instance, was universally accepted as a desirable moral trait. Not in postmodernism. In particular, it attacks the use of classifications such as male versus female, straight versus gay, white versus black, and imperial versus colonial.	The Simpsons (TV show), Fredric Jameson, Jean-Francois Lyotard	Chapters 1, and 24

AMERICAN & WORLD HISTORY

— High School History —

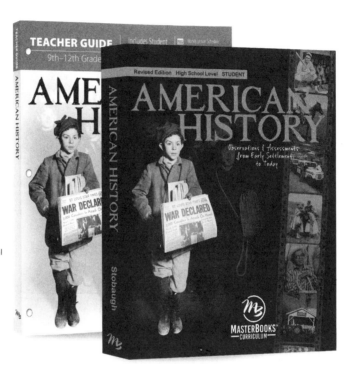

AMERICAN HISTORY
GRADE 9-12 *[1 YEAR / 1 CREDIT]*

Survey the history of America from native peoples, European settlements, nation-building, and expansion through the modern age. Actively build your student's strong biblical worldview, learning the political and faith perspectives that have impacted its history and cultural changes over time.

WORLD HISTORY
GRADE 9-12 *[1 YEAR / 1 CREDIT]*

Students will develop a Christian worldview while forming their own understanding of world history trends, philosophies, and events. Examinations of historical theories, terms, and concepts.

JACOBS' ELEMENTARY ALGEBRA

A Respected Standard for Teaching Algebra - Now New and Improved

This high school algebra curriculum provides a full year of math in a clearly written format with guidance for teachers as well as for students who are self-directed. The primary student text is divided into 17 sections, covering functions and graphs, integers, rational numbers, exponents, polynomials, factoring, fractions, and more. As the student works through the text, select solutions are provided in the text, with full answers available in the solutions manual.

Elementary Algebra	978-0-89051-985-1
Solutions Manual	978-0-89051-987-5
Teacher Guide	978-0-89051-986-8
3-BOOK SET	**978-0-89051-988-2**
Elementary Algebra DVD	713438-10237-5
3-BOOK / 1-DVD SET	978-1-68344-038-3

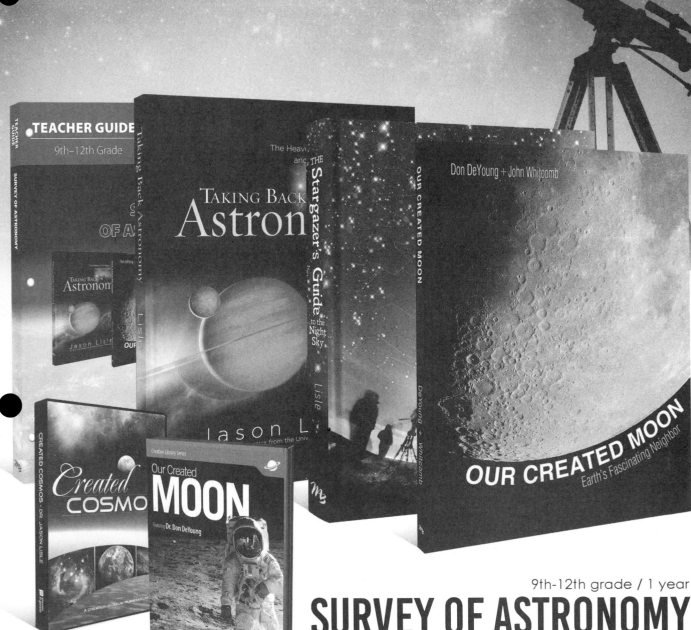

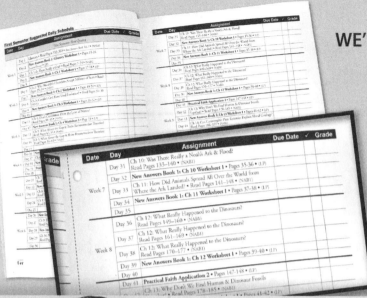